G000154398

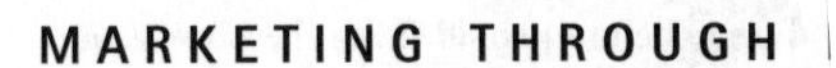
MARKETING THROUGH

To my grandmother who passed away before I could finish the book. *Lala ngoxolo ntombi kaMvundlane.*
To Ntombi, Ma, Mawe and Basheerah and all my friends and relatives who were there when I needed them.
To the scores of clients who had the faith to use my services in both research and advertising, and the hundreds of respondents who let me into their private lives.
And, last but not least, to my friend Prea Pillay, who passed away. May your soul rest in peace.

MARKETING THROUGH MUD AND DUST

MUZI KUZWAYO

ISBN 0 86486 452 3

First published in 2000 by Ink Inc
an imprint of
David Philip Publishers
208 Werdmuller Centre,
Newry Street,
Claremont, 7708

Designed and typeset by Stefanie Krieg-Elliott
Printed by Creda Communication, Eliot Avenue, Epping II, Cape Town

ELECTRICITY FOR SALE

FOREWORD

There are two rules to writing a foreword for a book. Firstly, don't gush about it or else the readers will think you're just doing a slick PR job. Secondly, don't steal the author's thunder by writing a long homily of your own views on the topic.

I find it difficult not to break the first rule. The book is a riveting read from start to finish – not only because it gives you some serious clues about marketing to black consumers (actually consumers generally), but because it is also raw, humorous and full of memorable punch lines. I'll let you, the reader, discover these nuggets for yourself but I have to mention one: 'Marketing is like a one-sided marriage. Only one party has to make it work and that is the marketer.' So wake up all you companies that believe in consumers flocking to you spontaneously.

The second rule is easy to obey. No one is going to upstage Muzi, least of all me. He wacks you with fresh insights and examples on every page. He never pulls his punches. Much of what he says is plain commonsense. So all I'd like to do is summarise a few of his favourite themes as an apéritif to the main course:

- So many marketing opportunities are waiting to be snapped up, if only a company is prepared to study the average day in the average life of a black consumer and research what he or she really wants;
- social gatherings, weddings and funerals have their traditional side but are changing in important ways too. Merchandisers need to be sensitive to the way informal socials and formal ceremonies are evolving;
- the channels for distributing goods and services into black communities are extremely varied and necessitate

very different marketing strategies for getting your brand on the shopping list;

- the first prize is to be the first-in and No. 1 brand in your category. But that can be undermined by extending the brand to other products; confusing the brand with the name of the company owning it; and being inconsistent over time with the positioning of the brand in the market. Sometimes it pays to keep the same image and the same, simple by-line through thick and thin;
- if you're launching a new brand, choose the name and slogans carefully bearing in mind that South Africa is multi-lingual and the words may have unintended nuances in other languages. Don't be overly politically correct;
- quality and reasonable pricing are now givens so that your product has to offer something more in the ads. Sometimes, word of mouth can be as powerful as advertising and it costs nothing;
- brand building now requires more than advertising. You have to get into the community with specific campaigns that foster lasting relationships;
- advertising is to sell products, not to win awards; and
- social campaigns such as AIDS awareness must have the same level of accountability as a normal consumer product campaign. If the message isn't getting through, the agency should be replaced.

But read on and get stuck into the real thing. You won't be disappointed.

CLEM SUNTER

INTRODUCTION

Black people constitute the largest group in South Africa. One would think that every marketer is aware of that, yet as recently as 1996 most main-stream supermarkets were refusing to stock black hair-care products and cosmetics – 'They didn't think there was a market for them'. By doing so they shut themselves out of a market that was then valued at over R500 million; current estimates are nearer to R600 million.

Every day of my working life I am a bouncing board for the ideas of creatives, strategic planners and clients: 'How do black people view this? Will black people find this funny? Is this insulting?' That's what made me think about writing this book. If I had written it earlier, maybe TBWA Hunt Lascaris would never have produced a commercial based on the concept of *ilobolo* for a sack of maize meal, offending millions of blacks in the process. And the agency probably would still be handling the account. And many such ads would never have been produced by mainly white agencies.

I doubted the need for the book until an Afrikaner ex-colleague came to me and said: 'You know, Muzi, I grew up in the Karoo, and I have never worked with black people before. I've known you people as maids and garden boys. All my childhood I was told you people are stupid, and every day I am surprised . . .' I liked his honesty and the way in which he acknowledged his mis-education. But what worried me was that clients had entrusted him with big budgets to market their products in the black community.

The time was January 1996. It was the Africa Cup of Nations Tournament and South Africa was the host. During those days there was more soccer in the air than oxygen. My colleague took a break from his favourite sport, rugby, to watch soccer for the first time. He found the game boring but the players fascinating, especially the white players. 'I wonder how those guys survive in the midst of so many blacks? I would be scared to death,' he told me.

Of course, not all white advertising practitioners and marketers are 'scared' of blacks. Many have worked, hugged and kissed 'them'. Yet how many have jumped into taxis, buses and trains to go to work with 'them'? How many understand 'their' lifestyle?

The black market is by no means static. There are now more BMWs in the township than before. There are more blacks in upmarket suburbs than before. More black and white children go to the same schools. Yet musicians like U2 and Genesis still sell more to whites than to blacks. And Babyface, Mdu, TKZee and 2PAC sell more to blacks than to whites.

Could this be a summary of things incomprehensible?

I've divided this book into three sections. In the first, Living in the Black, I take a journey through the backyards, streets and passageways of the township to give you an insight into our lives. You will meet the respondents I talked to while doing research for life assurance, oil, cigarette, liquor and car companies to mention but a few, as well as those I spoke to for the purposes of this book.

If you live in the township, or grew up there, you'll most probably find the safari back into childhood nostalgic, and the difference made by things such as age fascinating.

The second section, Heroes and Victims, looks at ways of building successful brands by learning from both those that succeeded and analysing the mistakes of those that failed. Some people will find this section uncomfortable because it is part of South African business culture not to criticise the high and mighty. When marketing strategies and advertisements fail to bring results they tend to blame everything from unfavourable weather to incompetent politicians to unfair competition. I also look at the reasons why some black empowerment companies failed at the first hurdle. But as traditional healers will tell you, if you are ill and want to be cured, you must be prepared to use something as uncomfortable as an enema up your bottom.

The last section, Cleaning the Cobwebs, looks at ways of writing effective communication and of being culturally sensitive.

I have avoided the kind of nonsense that I was told by some researchers when I first started working in advertising. One researcher told me that black people didn't like green in their advertising because it denotes bad luck.

'Really?' I asked.

'Yes! Didn't you know that?' she asked.

'No,' I replied, 'because the African National Congress's colours are black, green and gold. And green is a colour that is common to many other African flags.'

She didn't reply. She turned red, and never spoke to me again.

So, this book is aimed at white market researchers, advertisers and their agencies who say the most ridiculous things about us. But above all, it is aimed at those genuine business people who want to know how to market effectively to their consumers. And talk to them with the respect that is due to all human beings. But this book is also aimed at all those people who lived through the era of consumer boycotts and became aware of the buying power of blacks.

Naturally, in the long run, I hope this book will benefit black people too. Because nothing is more painful than the tasteless and sometimes insulting advertising that bursts uninvited into our homes.

I also hope that it will make us realise that in all areas of empowerment, marketing is probably the last field where we should expect businesses to redress past imbalances in a benevolent way. This is because advertising and marketing are by their very nature ruthless. Companies are competing for the same market and the same money. Not only in South Africa and not only between black and white, but in the rest of the world between white and white, black and white, black and black and all other shades in between. So, British Airways never made it easy for Virgin Airlines to get into the British airline market and Pepsi didn't rely on Coca-Cola's empathy to become their number two. A lesson Pepsi South Africa should have heeded.

In South Africa black people have the biggest advantage because they know the country's marketing terrain very well. Any guerrilla who knows the terrain is deadly.

Lastly, the facts that you'll find in this book are unashamedly subjective. I chose not to follow the rules of statistics, means and averages. They're too rigid. I preferred the wisdom of custom, instinct and culture because they make it easy to understand those irrational and sometimes accidental factors that elude scientific analysis and exact calculation yet affect business. Nor do I not claim to be a black expert. No one can accurately predict the behaviour and reaction of 40 million people. I am a marketing tour guide. I take you through the streets of townships to give you a glimpse of black life as I have lived it, as seen with my own brown eyes.

SECTION I
LIVING IN THE BLACK

1

A grandmother celebrating her ninetieth birthday with her 'family'.

Chapter 1

THE BLACK FAMILY

'*Umuntu akalahlwa*' goes an African adage, which means that 'a human being cannot be thrown away'.

'Ntate moholo' and 'Bab' Omkhulu', directly translated, mean 'senior father' in Sesotho and Zulu respectively. This is how a black child addresses his or her father's elder brother. 'Ntate' or 'Baba' is how they refer to their biological fathers; and 'rangoane', or 'baba omncane', or 'tata omncinci' (in Xhosa) to their father's younger brother, meaning junior father. However, many don't even use the appropriate prefix. They use the term 'father' regardless of their status to their father. There are equivalent terms that refer to the womenfolk like 'mangoane', 'mamncane' and 'mam omncinci' for junior mother, or 'mamogolo' and 'mamkhulu' for senior mother.

In Africa, a family is more than merely the sum of two biological parents.

Attend a family gathering and you'll be introduced to people you've never heard of before, and you'll be told that 'you are family, and you must take care of one another'. In many instances a family includes parents, grandparents, grandchildren, uncles, aunts, nephews and nieces. This meaning of 'family' has caused problems for life assurers and medical aid companies. One of the women I spoke to told me that she struggled for years to get life assurance cover for her aunts and cousins. Fortunately, some big life assurers responded to the difference in understanding of what the term 'family' constitutes and have recently launched policies such as Old Mutual's Flexi-Family Cover.

SLEEPER COUCHES AND HOTELS

Many township houses are small and there is little privacy. A phrase such as 'you're invading my space' is unheard of unless, of course, you are one of the privileged few. It is common for people not to have a bed of their own. A manager of a top German company told me that he had his first bed at university. Before that he had to 'sleep with' with his cousins and nephews.

He was luckier than Charles, a former class-mate of mine. Charles was one of those strange but common characters in the township. He owned an old Volvo which he had inherited from his grandfather. That made him one of only two pupils who owned a car at our school. He dressed exquisitely in his double-breasted jackets, imported trousers and expensive white Italian shirts which to him were ordinary school shirts.

Girls liked Charles. And so we called him 'Prince Charles'. But after he slept with a girl we greatly feared and admired, he was crowned and became King Charles.

But this king's throne had its limits. He lived in his parents' small, semi-detached house. He had neither a bedroom nor a bed. According to his friends, he slept on the floor in the dining-room. His mother detested his playboy habits because of the younger children in the family who saw him sleeping with different girls there.

I was luckier than Charles as far as the bed was concerned. I had my own. For a long time, there were only four of us at home, namely, Mawe,[1] Gogo,[2] Godna and me. Godna had his own bedroom inside the house, and I slept on a sleeper-couch in the kitchen outside the main house. It had a coal stove which made it feel like a palace in winter.

My luck ended whenever my older cousin, Freddie, came to visit from Soweto. Then I would have to share my sleeper-couch with him. And like King Charles, he was a lady's man.

Our circumstances were different to Charles's. Gogo and

Mawe were very strict. So Freddie could only bring his girlfriends over at night, and smuggle them out before dawn. The first time he brought a woman with him, I got up to sleep in the main house. He pleaded with me not to go because Gogo would then know what was happening in the outside kitchen. So for his libido's sake, I stomached every sound – the moaning, the groaning and the snoring that followed. Under those circumstances, it is only human to react. And I did it well. I waited for Freddie to fall asleep, then stealthily, very stealthily, pulled the blankets away from them. 'Good,' I thought, 'they'll get cold.'

A friend, Ray, once told me about how unlucky he was. He also had a strict mother who always warned him about unwanted pregnancies. If she heard him entering the house with a girl at night, she woke up immediately.

'My girl,' she would start, 'you are wasting your time with Ray. There are many girls who are crying because of him. He is a heart-breaker. I know him. I am his mother. He is going to dump you. What makes you think you are different from the rest? Take my advice. Go back home.'

Ray didn't stop. Beating the system was part of the thrill. So he devised a plan. 'We take our steps simultaneously. When I put my right foot forward, you do the same. When I put my left foot forward, you do the same.' You can't walk fast like that, but the irritation was worth the benefit. His plan worked for a while, until Ray's mother caught them doing the slow walk. Annoying as that was, Ray's mother couldn't summon the energy to scold them; she just laughed.

'What has this got to do with marketing?' you may ask. A lot. There is a company that is profiting from the lack of beds and bedrooms in the townships. Although I doubt whether it was ever the intention of the company to do so.

I was led to that story by chance. It was at a bus-stop and a woman was complaining about her ex-boyfriend. Being a researcher, I eavesdropped. 'He wanted us to sleep on the kitchen floor. I told him straight. You either take me to a hotel or you take me back home.'

'Is that the place to take a woman these days?' I asked her.

At first the two women were taken aback. They hadn't realised that there was someone listening to their conversation. Knowing that I had nothing to lose, I pressed on gently.

Eventually they told me. They also told me how inexpensive the hotel was. I followed the story further. I visited one of the hotels they were talking about. The receptionist told me he checked in a lot of locals. 'What does a man who lives in Diepkloof want at a hotel that's ten minutes away from home?' he asked me.

'You tell me,' I replied.

'Think for yourself,' he countered.

This is a typical example of people using a product for something other than what the marketer had envisaged. It is important to note that not every woman sleeps out, nor does every man bring a woman home. But for many houses, sleeping arrangements are problematic. And that alone is an opportunity for many marketers, including sleeper-couch manufacturers. They should easily be outselling sofas.

EXTENSIONS AND PARENTS

An extended family has very little disposable income because the money is shared by a larger number of people. This affects buying behaviour.

'I usually buy in bulk,' said a woman I spoke to about shopping habits. 'I have a big family. Six grandchildren and two children. And we all live together. Happily,' she emphasised.

A few blocks down the street in a different supermarket, I approached three young women who introduced themselves as sisters. Their trolley was so full you would have thought they were doing Christmas shopping. It was filled with staple foods such as samp, milk and mealie-meal. 'Am I also invited to the party?' I asked. 'No. We're not having a party. We're doing our fortnightly shopping,' she replied.

As I spent more time with them, I discovered that although they had introduced themselves as sisters, the third one was in fact a cousin, according to Western definitions. But because they had grown up in the same house, they considered her to be their sister. They also told me that their family was big with more brothers, sisters, nephews, nieces and an aunt. Dependants are therefore not necessarily your own offspring, but anyone who relies on your income and anyone who is part of the household.

Family members who get an education and/or good jobs are usually expected to help uplift the rest of the family. This may include paying for the education of their brothers, sisters, nephews and nieces.

Families that can afford it usually extend their houses by adding more rooms, even back rooms. As family members grow up and some leave home, back rooms can be rented out to tenants.

Tebogo of Soweto has a dream that haunts him day and night. 'I want to extend my parents' house,' he told me several times. 'That is the best gift I can ever give them to say thank you for raising me and educating me.'

He is not the only one.

Mike and his sister grew up orphans. He was raised by his Mamogolo,[3] along with her other children. As the first graduate in the family, he took care of his nephews and nieces who were still at school. These included not only his sister's children, but those of his cousins as well. In addition to that he bought a house for his sister and her three children. If he hadn't done that he would have bought his house and BMW much sooner.

Vusi, an accountant, bought a house for his parents before buying himself a brand new car. He said the reason why he did it was that he didn't want to be a laughing stock among his peers. He told me of a guy who lives in upmarket Houghton while his parents live in an overcrowded matchbox house.

'Taking care of one's parents is applauded in the black society. The concept of old-age homes is still despised by many.' This is what Refiloe, a respondent in one of my research groups, said. '[Old-age homes] are like hives where people who are finished with life are kept. Leaving my mother at an old-age home would be like leaving her at the waiting-room for death.'

Children of the same household share even the head of a locust.

– African Proverb

'But what if you're too busy to take care of her?' I asked. The answer came from another respondent. 'Wouldn't you pay for putting your parents at the old-age home? So you might as well use that money to employ someone to take care of them in your own house.' In every group that I ran, both men and women agreed on that point.

'How can you make such generalisations?' I asked them, 'especially because we know about things such as witchcraft between and within families in the black community? And witchcraft is a result of hatred and jealousy.'

The most eloquent answer came from a man who was in one of my groups in Durban. 'Every rule has exceptions, Muzi. But they are that – exceptions. If I were to tell you that as a rule black South Africans are forgiving people, will you disagree? Sure you can point out people who hate whites. But how many are they? If they were in the majority, we would have had a racial war. By the same token, I say the majority of black people take care of one another.'

A friend told me he once experienced this. He interviewed a guy for a job and asked him to come back the next day for a second interview. 'No, I can't make it tomorrow,' replied the guy, 'because my brother needs the suit that I'm wearing now to go for his job interview.' This benevolence seldom extends to 'luxury' items such as cigarettes and alcohol. People share only with people who are willing to buy. Free-loaders are avoided.

SINGLE MOTHERS

You know them, those girls who fall pregnant before they know what the word sex means. And the women who don't want men in their lives but want their children? The good wives who are deserted by their husbands, and the fiancées who are jilted after engagement? You meet them in taxis, or see them in their cars as they drive to their townhouses. Some of them still live in the townships, and they take care of their children as well as those of other family members.

As a collective, these women have purchasing power. In fact, they constitute a market segment on their own. Needless to say, their needs are different and, although they have similar interests to the rest of us, empathising with their unique situation will surely grab their attention.

MARKETING CONSIDERATIONS

- A family is usually more than just two parents and their offspring. It involves relatives as well.
- Money is shared by a number of people, except for luxuries.
- Disposable income is usually less than in white households but the sheer number of people justifies marketing to this group.
- Single mothers have purchasing power and deserve attention from marketers.

2

**Many live on the edge.
Perhaps our communication should
reveal this simple truth.**

Chapter 2

A WEEK IN THE LIFE . . .

MORNING

As the sun rises over the mixture of mist and dust in the township, taxis, buses and trains have long started making their way to town[1] where most people work. Those who own cars have the luxury of following a little later, as well as listening to their car radios.

Let's talk about those who use public transport. They are the furthest from the boardroom, and the least understood. I enjoy public transport. I like the camaraderie, the singing, the preaching, the praying and the jesting. This is the birthplace of ideas.

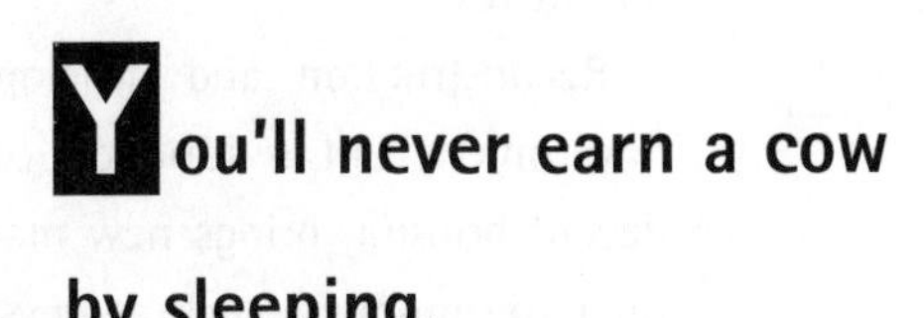
You'll never earn a cow
by sleeping.

– African adage

Townships are generally far from town. This was deliberately planned by the architects of apartheid. As early as 4:00 a.m. streets fill up with people going to work. Among them are mothers who leave while their children are asleep. There is no time to prepare a big breakfast. Many rely on a cup of coffee or tea and a few slices of bread. Mothers with younger children will at least prepare mealie-meal or sorghum porridge for them to eat before going to school.

Some parents have no choice but to leave the children alone to prepare themselves for school. In these cases, it is usually the responsibility of the eldest to ensure that the younger siblings are washed, fed and clothed. If they are too young, they're taken to an unemployed neighbour or pensioner who'll take care of them. Babies are left with a child-minder in the neighbourhood. Those with the means, employ one from the rural areas to live with them.

Liberation has resulted in many people moving to areas

where they have no relatives, and into neighbourhoods that have largely young people. Neighbours do not know one another well enough to leave children. This has resulted in a boom in crèches and nursery schools.

Many parents also don't have time to teach their children basic hygiene such as brushing their teeth and eating healthily. They rely on schools to teach that. This must be a priority for schools, as well as for pharmaceutical companies, detergent manufacturers and any other companies involved in personal or public hygiene.

Although many houses have been electrified in recent years, few have bathrooms, and even fewer have hot water. Houses that don't have electricity use coal, primer stoves or gas stoves.

Reconstruction and development is not a function of government but a function of marketing. Think about it, decent housing brings new markets and creates opportunity for more products such as geysers, furniture, appliances, etc. Manufacturers should also look at growing their markets by inventing new products and product categories. What good is technology if it cannot improve our quality of life?

DURING THE DAY

At this time most of the working people have left for work. Taxis to industrial areas are fewer because there are fewer passengers. This makes it difficult for people who have to attend job interviews in those areas.

When arranging a job interview, some black managers make it a point to find out if the candidate has a car. If he or she does not, then the interview is held between seven and eight in the morning or late afternoon between four and five. This gives the candidate a chance to catch a taxi back to the township. Just as empowerment is nothing without improvement, affirmative action is nothing without empathy.

In the early afternoon school children start trickling back home. They do the chores such as cleaning and cooking. During this time, media consumption is largely in the form of radio. Unlike newspapers or TV, a radio playing the latest hits makes a good companion while you clean. Favourite DJs are on air around this time and the parents are not at home to complain about irritating or loud music.

The many commercial breaks during the late-afternoon soapies allow people to check their pots!

Late afternoon, when the cleaning is finished, soapies start on television. 'Food burns' as the saying goes, because people watch them while doing their cooking. One respondent told me that the reason why there are so many commercial breaks during soapies is to allow people to check their pots. (It's amazing what people who don't understand advertising think.)

Soapies are powerful. People talk about them as if the actors are their scandalous neighbours. There have been instances where the local actors have been beaten up in real life for the roles they play on television.

Soaps can become an excellent vehicle for advertisers. Instead of having a soap star endorsing a brand in a commercial, you could have the brands used in the soap or sponsoring a programme. Marketers can contribute towards the making of the films, and our nascent film and TV industries will be able to compete with overseas-produced material.

PRIME TIME

'Darkness will bring you back!' is what my grandmother would say as I ran away from her during the day. It is an African saying, *kuyokuqoqa ukuhlwa,* often used by parents when a child runs away for fear of punishment.

Many families are strict about the time at which a child should come back at night. As a rule of thumb, when the street lights are turned on, most gates are locked, and viewers become glued to their television sets. This, however, is also time for boys to 'check' or to 'collect half promises'. Checking is a colloquial term meaning to visit one's girlfriend, while collecting half promises is when the girl being courted tells one whether or not she is willing to be one's girlfriend.

In the township that can be challenging. Firstly, most parents are strict with their daughters and therefore boys dare not enter a girl's home. He has to stand outside and hope that she will come out to 'check' if he has arrived while maintaining a certain presence in the house for the parents to think that she is still inside.

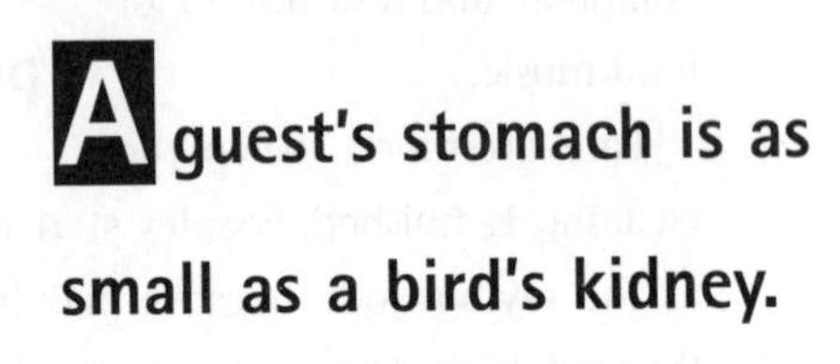

A guest's stomach is as small as a bird's kidney.
– African proverb

Couples who have phones have it easy. They can phone and make an appointment. A cellphone makes life even easier. But most people do not have phones.

In these circumstances, an outside toilet is an asset. She can visit it often without arousing too much suspicion. A house with no tap inside is also a blessing in this case because she can go out as if she is fetching a glass of water. Then if she sees him, she will quickly go back inside the house, 'check the score' and dash to talk to her loved one, and, hopefully, get a kiss or two.

Sometimes the girl being courted won't come out. Then the courter either has to whistle or send a child to call her for him.

Sending a child is no guarantee of success. Most parents do not separate the messenger from the sender. Anyway, back to prime time . . .

This is the time to read the newspaper, have supper and watch television. It's also the time for the family to catch up. This is probably the best time to reach your audience via electronic media. It is also the time to prepare for the morning rat race, for example, choosing what to wear the following day.

WEEKENDS

On weekends people have more time. The queues to buy *vetkoek* are longer and there is more time to prepare maize-meal porridge. The middle to upper income groups prepare more expensive cereals for breakfast. They have the money to buy them throughout the month anyway.

Saturday morning is time to clean, do the laundry and shop, especially in town. Car radios compete with home music centres as both houses and cars are cleaned. But if there's a funeral nearby it becomes so quiet even the stones seem to be mourning.

The weekend is also a time to engage in social activities such as sport, weddings, funerals, taverns and parties. Those who don't want to be seen in shebeens organise their own get-togethers, such as sit-ins and street bashes.

Early Sunday morning is a treat for gossip mongers. They get to see who went to sleep with whom the previous night because that is when girls come back from a 'sleep out' with their boyfriends. Parents hate it when their daughters sleep out, and girls have become experts at outsmarting their parents. One of the famous disguises is wearing a morning gown. The girl takes it with her to the boyfriend's house and wears it the following morning when she returns home. The idea is that her parents will think that she probably just stepped outside. Some even wear Eskamel, which is a facial mask.

When you see adult women putting shawls on their shoulders, men wearing jackets and a girl following a few metres behind, you know there is trouble. Someone is pregnant. And they are going to report the matter to the boyfriend's parents.

'Your dog has eaten our chicken's eggs,' the leader of the entourage will say after introducing themselves. That means 'your son has made our daughter pregnant'. This is called *icala* in Zulu or *molato* in Sesotho, which means 'charge'. The culprit or boyfriend is then called and asked how he pleads. If he pleads guilty, then his family has to pay 'damages'. If the boy pleads *not* guilty, which often happens, then the girl's parents leave. There is a belief that if you deny that you are the father, the baby will be born looking exactly like the father. I think it is true.

Many radio stations play jazz and choral music on Sunday mornings. South Africa is a religious country and many people listen to church services on radio. But let's skip church. In the afternoon the fun continues – social activities, stokvels, societies and more weddings.

MARKETING CONSIDERATIONS

- Commuting from the townships forces people to leave home early and come back late, making it difficult to prepare healthy meals.
- Liberation has resulted in many people moving to areas where they have no relatives or into neighbourhoods largely inhabited by young people. This has resulted in a boom in crèches and nursery schools.
- Many parents don't have enough time to teach their children things like basic hygiene. Companies have a social responsiblity in this regard and should take a long-term view on social investment.
- Products are always needed in the townships that will improve the quality of life.

3

Young though they may be, black children exert a strong influence on the success of certain brands.

Chapter 3

THE POWER OF CHILDREN

Black South African children have always had influence, from politics to groceries. . .

Most black families can't afford 'helpers' or domestic workers, so chores are divided among family members. Children come home earlier than their parents and are expected to clean and cook.

In a family where there are both boys and girls, the latter usually clean the house and the former do the garden and clean the yard. In others, everyone does the chores. Many people applaud boys for doing girls' chores.

Blacks dislike using words such as 'maid', 'domestic worker' and 'nanny'. These are associated with madams and using them demeans their own people. The preferred term is 'helper'.

One of the children's duties is to buy the groceries – especially on weekends. This puts the fate of many FMCG[1] brands in their hands. They are the ones who go to shops and spazas, and in many cases decide which brands to buy. Take Nana and Sindi, for example, who are 7 and 10 years old respectively. They had a shopping list which was drawn up by their mother. This is how it read: omo, milk, eggs, colgate and shoe polish. (Omo and Colgate have become generic names, which is why they are in small letters.)

In other words Nana and Sindi's shopping list didn't have any brand names. Still, the chances of buying the Omo and Colgate brands are high because they own top-of-mind awareness. As for the eggs, milk and shoe polish the girls decided which brand to buy.

You could argue that in most cases children know which brands their parents prefer. However, that brand may be out of stock and the parent will not be there to be consulted on the substitute. So, unless the child is under strict orders not to buy an alternative, they decide which product to buy. Furthermore, the high degree of illiteracy among parents contributes to children introducing new products to their families.

Sometimes a boss's and a deputy's interests clash. This also occurs between mother and child in supermarket matters. For instance, in the case of cleaning products children prefer products that will help them finish their chores quickly so that they can go and play or visit friends. Parents, on the other hand, want products that will do the job well. And children come up with all sorts of excuses for buying their favoured products or brands.

It should be noted, however, that the division of labour in the home influences future behaviour of non-core target markets. For instance, young men who live on their own, either in hostels or flats, soon find themselves using soap powder, detergents as well as other product such as porridge, pasta or floor-polish that were used in their home when they were growing up. It is therefore important to target a wide range of family members and to remember that families, rather than the individual, may have developed strong loyalties to certain brands.

MARKETING CONSIDERATIONS

- Most families cannot afford domestic workers, so children do the chores.
- Children have a great influence in the purchasing decision.
- Products should communicate with a wide range of people in the family.

4

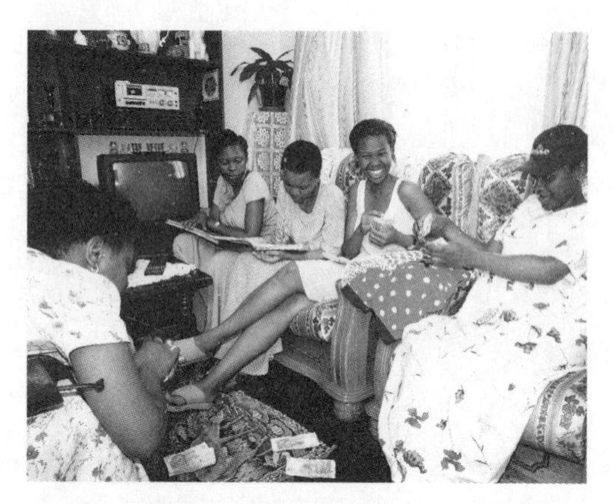

These women are sharing the proceeds of their 'society' at the end of the year. Such savings schemes lead to large sums of cash circulating among people.

Chapter 4

SOCIAL GATHERINGS

WHEN WE WERE BANTUS

In the past blacks were forbidden to drink clear beer and spirits or 'European alcohol' as it was called. We were allowed to drink only what was then called 'kaffir beer'. We were also forbidden to enter bottle stores.[1] Entrepreneurial white hobos made good business from this. They would stand outside the bottle store waiting for blacks who wanted to buy European alcohol. And they demanded good pay for their services. If you couldn't afford it, as the story goes, Baas Hobo would drink half of whatever you bought.

Even though we were allowed to drink 'kaffir beer', brewing it was forbidden. We could only buy it from government-owned beer halls. Only men were allowed in beer halls. As far as our white, Christian government was concerned, black women weren't allowed to drink. But in fact they did, as they still do today. Traditionally the women brew the beer.

Pro-family activists will hate this: most drinking males prefer to spend their spare time with friends, away from the wife, family and chores.

They couldn't be stopped. They brewed underground. And shebeens[2] were born. To beat the system, the ever-ingenious entrepreneurs employed people to dig holes to hide the beer. A person who dug such a hole was called *'isimba mgodi'* which means a hole digger. It now means anyone who works at a shebeen or tavern.

There was a police unit called the 'liquor squad'. Their duty was to raid shebeens, confiscate the liquor and arrest all the patrons, including visitors. If you wanted to throw a party, you were supposed to get permission from the local police captain, who was always white, of course. And in most instances you had to bribe him.

Drunk with power, the Nats hurt the liquor companies as much as the drinkers. After intense lobbying, the government allowed blacks to drink clear beer as from August 1962. But drinking spirits was forbidden until later.

Then blacks were allowed to buy from bottle stores but had to use separate entrances from white people. This made shebeens thrive despite the police raids.

Later, blacks were allowed to own bottle stores. And these became money spinners. A licence to own one was a licence to print money. Only few licences were issued, and there were always allegations of bribery. But no one could object in public because white officials were involved.

Liquor producers found another problem – bottle-necking at bottle stores. They depended on only a few bottle stores. The police continued raiding shebeens, which was where most of the liquor was consumed. Liquor companies continued to lobby. For the first time shebeen owners could apply for licences to own taverns, buy directly from liquor companies and not have their stock confiscated. Liquor companies now send their reps to visit taverns.

Taverns hurt bottle stores just as spazas hurt the general dealers. They have become big channels of distribution.

TYPES OF TAVERNS

There are several names that refer to places of drinking and they differ from province to province and from region to region. But words like tavern, shebeen, spot and joint (in KwaZulu-Natal) are the most common.

There are generally two types of tavern. The first one is where people buy and sit. These vary from beautiful settings visited by the cream of the township to dark and dingy ones. The second type of tavern is where people buy their stuff and move to other places such as parties, sit-ins, stokvels or street bashes.

Some taverns are more than just channels of distribution; visiting them portrays a certain image as well. There are taverns where top 'ouens' and 'top ousies' are seen, and that is where your product must be seen to capture the local market.

OTHER DRINKING PLACES

There is a high consumption of alcohol at private homes simply because some consumers don't want to be seen to be drinking at shebeens. This is what bra[3] Mandla said: 'We didn't grow up drinking in joints. Joints are not for us. In fact it's not right for a person of my calibre to be seen at a joint. I am a school principal.'

'So where do you drink?' I asked him.

'Like I said to you earlier, I buy my whisky on Saturday mornings or beginning of the month, and drink it either at my house or at a friend's place. Sometimes I go out to a park with them, and enjoy it there. But you will never ever catch my black bones in a tavern.'

Lindiwe, a professional woman, had this to say: 'You know people have a certain perception of you if you drink in a tavern. I'd say a bad perception. So we prefer to buy our stuff in town and have a sit-in with friends or go to a kitchen party or stokvel or something like that . . .'

'I don't think it's right for a woman to go to a shebeen,' Lebo said.

'And to a tavern?' I asked.

'What's the difference?' she asked.

Some people don't want to be seen in taverns.

SIT-INS

A sit-in or cool sit-in is a get-together of a group of friends and acquaintances who come together to enjoy music and drink. It is exclusive and classy because you attend only by invitation.

STREET BASHES

Street bashes are parties held in the street. Go there and you'll find guys talking on their cellphones more than dancing to the music. They are show-off places. Unlike in a club or tavern, here everyone can see the car you drive. You can talk on your cellphone without being labelled a braggart. It's outside after all. Never mind that it's very hard to hear the person you're talking to. Street bashes are totally an image thing. Brands are here today and gone tomorrow. This is where the latest brands are seen or scorched.

'*Yo. Na lo sekaphuza lento. Angisayifuni*,' I've heard them mutter. 'Oh my goodness! Even this person drinks this? I don't want it any more.' This is a high-risk, high-gain environment. For new brands, it can be an excellent launch pad or a dreadful guillotine.

STOKVELS

'*Sisayo sapota usibanibani*' ('We're going to support so and so'). That's what people usually say when going to a stokvel.

A stokvel is a group of members who come together to help each other, either with food or money. It's a modernisation of the old, African concept of *ilima* or *lejema*. According to bra Bogie Mabogoane, an expert in black urban history, the word stokvel comes from the English word 'stock-fair'.

In the old days, when it was time to cultivate the fields, families would come together to form teams that would work in the fields of all the neighbouring households. This ensured that everyone reaped at harvest. Now because our economy has changed, reaping means making money.

At stokvels guests buy liquor and food to support the host. Neighbours and friends who may not be members of that particular stokvel also come to support the host.

TRADITIONAL CEREMONIES

Traditional ceremonies are an open invitation. The most common are initiation and sacrificial ceremonies. They involve slaughtering either a goat or a sheep. Some black Christians are opposed to these practices.

I have always been amazed by old people who tell me about traditions that involve spirits. No, I'm not talking about ancestors, ghosts or anything like that. I'm talking about brandy, whisky and vodka. For instance, in Xhosa tradition when an initiate comes back from circumcision in the bush, brandy must be available. And when sangomas dance in the Cape, the ceremony is not considered complete until there's a bottle of Smirnoff.

My cellphone rang.

It was my Sri Lankan-born friend, Ravi.

'Hi Ravi!'

'Where are you, Muzi?'

'I'm in Khayelitsha, we've just finished slaughtering a sheep'.

My mouth was full and he could tell.

'So what are you eating?'

'A penis,' I replied.

INSIDE A NO-MAN'S PARTY

'Please let me in,' I plead.

'No.'

'I promise to be totally unintrusive.'

'No.'

'Please.'

'What? Do you want a sign that says women only?'

'Why does he want to come into a kitchen party? Is he uncle, auntie or something?' another one asks.

'I am only doing marketing research. I want to know what your favourite brands are and how you do things.'

'Research. Research for whom?'

'For myself. I'm writing a book on advertising and marketing.'

'Come in,' she said, but as soon as she realised that I had a camera in my hand, she put a condition on my admission: 'Don't take any photographs.'

'No, I won't.'

'Put that camera away.'

'Okay, I'll buy you some drinks.'

'We don't want any of your drinks. Just put that camera away or leave.'

Those were the conditions laid down for me to get into kitchen parties, almost everywhere. I now know why they're so gender-exclusive. Nudity is not one of them. There's the exchanging of gifts and drinking. Some of the ladies walk in as total abstainers and leave with endless giggles.

Women at kitchen parties said exactly the same things as those in liquor focus groups. They drink just to enjoy themselves far from the prying eyes of men. In my entire life, I have never seen so much energy and joy as at kitchen parties.

I could never account for all the places where fun takes place. Every now and again new ones appear. But they seldom deviate completely from the established ones. Now there are bashes in places you would have never thought of. For instance, Savanna Dry hosted a Savanna Dry Kwaito revolution at the Rosebank Fire Station. Such venues are really hip, and tend to make it with the upmarket young blacks who can afford to attend them. But fun occurs everywhere: beaches, rooftops, parks, etc. I can't name them all. I only hope to cast a small ray of light on the countless opportunities that are in this seemingly dark forest called the black market, main market or whatever.

MARKETING CONSIDERATIONS

- Know the social status of various drinking places.
- Identify the right association for the brand especially for promotions. For example it wouldn't be right for J&B Whisky to be promoted at street bashes. 'Street bashes are for children', according to J&B drinkers.

5

A black wedding showing the same couple at different times of the day.

Chapter 5

THE BLACK WEDDING

Lead Vocals: *Makoti ke di nako, a hela oa gana na?*
[Bride, the time has come, or are you refusing now?]
Background: *Oa jeka, jeka.*
[You're hesitating, you're hesitating.]
This is what the groom's party chants as they fetch the bride from her parent's house. The bridal party replies with their own song poking fun at the groom:

'Betty, Betty, Hela mntwanami/Wangilethela umkhwenyana,/ngezinyawo ezinomnkenke/ Uyongidabulela amashidi.'

[Betty, Betty, my child/You're bringing me a son-in-law/ Who has rough heels./He is going to tear my sheets.]

Rehearsing the songs takes at least a week. Neither party wants to embarrass themselves in the presence of the other. It's the whole process of suitors again. Only this time families are involved.

The process starts with *ilobolo* or *magadi*, which signifies the start of a life-long relationship between the two families. Their other sons and daughters are now forbidden to marry one another, in the same way they can't marry their own brothers and sisters.

This procedure has strict rules, and any party that strays is usually fined anything from fifty cents to a bottle of brandy; and, depending on the gravity, it can be a whole cow. The groom's family will arrive on the set day and time. The gates may even be locked when they arrive to test their resilience, as well as to weaken their position before the negotiations begin. Then someone may come and ask for a small fee for the gates to be opened. To an outsider this may look like a money-making scheme. It's not that at all. Women are not for sale. This is an old prank to bring the two families together.

Once the groom's family is inside, the father of the bride-to-be might refuse to open his mouth. And another fee must be paid to get him to speak. This is called *imvulamlomo* – the mouth-opener. Thereafter negotiations start until the amount of *lobolo* is agreed upon. And the wedding date set. It's a long-winded process where people speak slowly and with pride. This is Africa, we have all the time in the world.

THE WEEK BEFORE THE WEDDING DAY

During the week of the wedding the bride's and groom's separate parties rehearse. There's singing and dancing throughout the week. The families also buy food and other necessities required to make the approaching wedding memorable. There is very little time to compare prices. The week is too short. So people buy at places such as wholesalers, which are perceived to be cheaper. Also, because of the large number of expected guests, it's better to buy in bulk. Flour, rice, mealie-meal, sugar, eggs, cooking oil, cold-drink, etc., fill the backs of vans. At home women brew traditional beer, bake biscuits and feed the guests. The week is not only about food, song and dance, there is also the hard work of spring cleaning the house, painting and cleaning the yard.

Weddings are expensive, especially because they are an open invitation – the neighbours, uncles, aunts and even the relatives who live on the other side of the earth attend. There are almost no hotels in townships. All the guests are accommodated by the families. Some are accommodated by neighbours and others by nearby relatives. Wherever they stay, most of them will sleep either on the floor or share beds. In townships houses are small. To augment them tents are hired. This is quite a good side-line business.

If it rains on your wedding day, it's believed that it's because the groom used to eat out of the pot when he was young. But if the sun shines, you'll see a sea of colour as Africans in either Western or traditional clothes raise their voices.

If it is a Western wedding, or 'white wedding' as it is called, the parties meet in church where the service has an Afro-Christian flavour. After the bride and his groom have been joined in matrimony, they are driven to the bride's home.

The songs and dances that were rehearsed during the week are performed amidst the ululation as the couple parade up and down the streets.

Later in the day the bride changes from the white wedding gown to traditional clothes or some other outfit. Then senior members of the family advise the parties on how to behave towards each other and towards relatives in their marriage. Wedding gifts such as bedding and furniture are presented to the newly-weds so they can start their new life.

On Saturday evening the bride is taken to the groom's family. And on Sunday morning the ceremony starts all over again. Now it's their turn to witness their son parading with his wife on the streets. It's also their turn to entertain their guests, neighbours, friends and relatives.

Late in the afternoon the bride is welcomed by her new family. Again old people advise them on how to behave towards each other and their respective families. Again wedding gifts are presented to the newly-weds. The wedding usually ends with the reception at night.

MARKETING CONSIDERATIONS

- Understand the idiosyncrasies of black weddings.
- Weddings are open to all and the family therefore buys in bulk to cater for all the visitors to their home.
- Accommodation and space are in short supply over the wedding period.

Concrete is poured into a grave to prevent the casket from being stolen.

Chapter 6

THE FUNERAL

Unlike weddings which occur with the consent of the parties concerned, death needs no permission and strikes at will. However, people can plan for their own death and for that of their relatives.

My grandmother never had a life assurance policy. Her cover was her five daughters and nephew. And as the grandchildren were born, her cover was increased. One of her daughters is a member of a 'society' – a group of neighbours, relatives or friends who assist each other if death strikes. Society members pay monthly subscription fees.

These societies are a cross between a 'life assurance' company and a stokvel. When a member loses one of the people he or she has covered, the society pays out. In addition to that, members assist with the cooking and all other work that is associated with funerals. This is why societies are so popular – 'they are the hands I will need'.

'The pain of being unable to pay for the funeral of your loved one is worse than death.'

– Respondent in a research group

In the old days people used to bury the deceased within days of their demise. But that was not agreeable to employers, so they stopped it. Now the corpse stays for a week or more at a mortuary. At a cost, of course.

Sometimes the funeral is delayed because close relatives who live far away must take time off from work so they can 'accompany their loved one'.

Preparations usually take a week. This includes buying a cow or sheep as well as food for the mourners. Like weddings, funerals are an open invitation. It is expected of neighbours to console the bereaved.

'Funerals have become a social gathering,' complained S'thembile to me. 'They are now a fashion parade where people show their latest designer wear from Parisian sunglasses to Italian footwear,' he continued.

'Funerals used to be dignified, a true last respect for the deceased. Now people go and see what the so-called bereaved have put on display. They look at the type of food that has been prepared, what salads, what drinks are available, what so and so is wearing, and what car they are driving . . . I know of a guy who doesn't go to funerals in his car because his friends tease him that he drives an appliance. A Daewoo. What sort of nonsense is that?' Phindi also complained.

'Funerals have become a time to show off your material well-being.'

– Respondent

'What made people lose respect for death and funerals were the killings in the eighties and early nineties,' Mabusha told me.

What they are saying is probably true. Funerals have changed from the sombre, dark 'last wedding' that they used to be, to a 'colourful display of fashion'. At the graveyard one often sees groups of 'mourners' talking and laughing loudly about other things. And after the funeral we now have 'after-tears', which is a party held in honour of the deceased. Such a thing was unheard of a few years ago.

'Death is death. It will always occur, broer. There is no need to bash our heads and cry as if it shouldn't happen to us or our loved ones. At funerals we normally meet old friends whom we haven't seen for years because they live in far-away places. So we might as well celebrate before we meet in grief again,' said Pat from Port Elizabeth. This caused a heated debate and bra Themba disagreed with him sharply: 'Just like you won't weep or mourn at a twenty-first, you can't *celebrate* the death of someone. That's my point.'

Indigenous culture and faiths are rooted in this country. People who practise them find in them what others find in their own religions – a solace from their daily misery and a promise of bliss in the next life. And as long as people experience hardships and dread evil spirits, the graves of their ancestors will continue to provide a comfortable refuge for them. It's better not to generate advertising material that mocks them.

Regardless of the 'modernisation' of many traditional ceremonies, do not mock indigenous beliefs – it can backfire badly.

MARKETING CONSIDERATIONS

- Many black families are careful to set money aside to pay for a decent funeral. However, there still is a big opportunity for life assurance in the black community.
- Funerals have changed over the years and have become more festive. They are also occasions to show off.
- Do not make fun of sangomas and ancestors. In spite of the changes in traditional ceremonies, many people still respect them.

7

Nike – now a fabric of society.

Chapter 7

A WORD FROM THE STREET

Name: KHOTSO

Muzi: Are you different from your white colleagues at school?

Khotso: Yes.

Muzi: What makes you different?

Khotso: Our interests. They keep together as whites, we do the same as blacks. Our interests are different. They play rugby and cricket. We don't play rugby.

Muzi: Who influences you?

Khotso: My uncle.

Muzi: Who influences other black kids?

Khotso: Their friends.

Muzi: What are your hopes?

Khotso: I want to have money.

Muzi: How will you make money?

Khotso: I don't know.

Muzi: What brands would you buy?

Khotso: Adidas, Carvella, Nike, DKNY and maybe Polo.

Name: LEBO

Muzi: Who is your role model?

Lebo: I'm my own role model.

Muzi: What makes you different?

Lebo: My approach to life. I'm positive – I know what I want and I'm optimistic. I don't give up.

Muzi: What do you have in common with your peers?

Lebo: Going out, being with friends and having money and buying great clothes.

Muzi: What brands do you like?

Lebo: T-shirts – no brand names. They are too expensive. But takkies must be Bronx. They are expensive but I must have them.

Muzi: And the future?

Lebo: I know I'll have a nice car, live in a townhouse. Doing advertising or public relations or be a saleswoman.

Muzi: Who influences others?

Lebo: Celebrities. They see them on TV.

Muzi: If you had lots of money?

Lebo: I'd leave South Africa. I want to see life from a different perspective. I mean I was born here, I grew up here. So now I want to see something different. I'd certainly be living in a townhouse. And then, I'd be driving a Pajero.

Name: VUSI

Muzi: What do you have in common with your peers?

Vusi: I don't know. I've always told myself that I'm different. Except for going to parties.

Muzi: What makes you different?

Vusi: I like to believe I'm more mature than the rest of them. Especially in things like taking care of the home, respecting other people's feelings in and outside the home, and having *ubuntu*.

Muzi: Do you think people have lost *ubuntu*?

Vusi: No, I don't think they've lost it. It's still within them. But they are neglecting it because of the European culture that is coming in.

Muzi: What is European culture?

Vusi: It is the culture that we black people are not familiar with. It is imposed on us through the media. We take it as it is without questioning because it promises us . . . what? Something we never had before.

Muzi: And your future plans?

Vusi: In ten years I'll be a board member of some radio station.

Muzi: Why radio station?

Vusi: I like communications and broadcasting. In the next five years I'll probably be a journalist or a news editor. There is nothing special about these jobs.

Muzi: Who influences you?

Vusi: No one in particular. But all mothers and fathers who are good mothers and fathers.

Muzi: What influences your peers?

Vusi: The rich and famous.

Muzi: Is that good or bad?

Vusi: Partly good and partly bad. Bad in that they look for money and forget about other things like giving your skills to the community for free. Going out to meet people and to museums, those are things that don't need any money. But it can be good because we all love money. And when you've got money, well . . .

Muzi: If you had lots money what would you buy?

Vusi: I'd invest half of it. Further my studies, uplift those around me and my family. And donate a portion to charity.

Names: KELE and ZAZA

Muzi: Who influences you? (No answer.) Who influences current trends?

K and Z: Americans like Aaliyah and others.

Muzi: What brands are hot today?

K and Z: Levi's, Diesel, Skechers, Kicks, Buffaloes, Free jeans from Edgars. There are so many, you know that!

Muzi: Which ones will always be there?

K and Z: Levi's will always be there. Free jeans? I'm not sure if it will be there for a long time. It's one of those that come and go. It's only found at Edgars.

Muzi: Your future plans?

K and Z: A car. A nice big house, but not too big. No kids.

Muzi: Why no kids?

K and Z: Ah! Ah! They're such a burden. You can't go anywhere anytime. It's not easy hanging around with your friends. You can't have a girl-talk anymore. And it means you already have a serious relationship with someone. Because there is this third person in your life.

Muzi: If you had lots of money?

K and Z: Levi's. Lots and lots of shoes. Bags and more jeans. A nice car. Nike jackets. Levi's tight jeans. Lots of silver jewellery.

Muzi: Why silver jewellery?

K and Z: It's nicer. Everyone wears gold jewellery. Including *tsotsis*. They wear gold teeth. Ah!

Muzi: What makes you different from your peers?

K and Z: We're independent. Unlike other people who are dependent on others to make their dreams come true.

Muzi: What do you have in common with others?

K and Z: We have little in common.

Muzi: What did you have in common with your white colleagues at school?

Kele: Nothing really. We all liked things like fun. But we always had problems at socials. We blacks couldn't enjoy socials because we used to fight about music with whites. They liked their own music and we liked ours. Whenever we wanted a song, we'd have to ask our teachers to talk to them. And even then they'd play you some stupid song from 1992 in 1997. We also liked different clothes. They liked white labels like Billabong. We were more with black brands like Fubu. Okay, we all liked brands like Tommy. We never liked the same things.

Muzi: Zaza?

Zaza: We never had a problem. We blacks were in the majority.

SECTION II
HEROES AND VICTIMS

8

The main channels of distribution for FMCGs.

Chapter 8

CHANNELS OF DISTRIBUTION FOR FAST-MOVING CONSUMER GOODS (FMCGs)

Channels for Fast Moving Consumer Goods (FMCG) are the general dealer, supermarket, spaza (and its variations), as well as the street vendor. Most of them buy their stock from wholesalers such as Metro Cash and Carry, and Jumbo.

THE GENERAL DEALER

The general dealer is a formal establishment which is usually situated centrally and within walking distance of the consumer's home. In the past, its centrality was its strength because of the large number of customers it could serve. But the proliferation of spaza shops has changed its fate.

THE SPAZA

'Spaza' means imitation. A spaza shop is usually attached to the owner's house. It can be anything from a garage, an outside room to a disused ship container. It is smaller than the general dealer and has an even smaller customer base. But that is its strength. It is a convenient convenience store. It is closer to its customers and its overheads are lower. One other factor which makes spazas successful is that the owner is often a neighbour. And in a community where neighbourliness is prized, this is a grand prize.

Counter-service stores are still predominant in townships. The shop assistant stands behind the counter and passes you whatever you ask for by name. And if the customer doesn't know it by name, as frequently occurs, he or she points at it.

The counter acts as a barrier between your customer and

your brand, and the shop-assistant is the almighty middleman. Do not think that all these assistants are helpful. I've heard them utter the famous township line '*Phuma la, uma ungayazi into oyifunayo!*' [Get out of here if you don't know what you want!]

Spaza's have an even bigger barrier. It is not just counter-service, but small-window burglar-proofed stand-on-a-platform-to-see-me service. Here there is no room for 'shelf decorators' as one spaza owner told me. Products must sell. Yes, spaza owners do take on new products. If you want them to stock it, it's only courteous to push it strongly through advertising.

Counter-service stores are still pedominant in the townships. So if a customer can't remember the brand name of a product, they can't ask for it!

While working on a snack project, I discovered that Simba Chips was the brand by far the most stocked by township retailers. I wanted to know why they didn't stock the nearest competitor. The answer was so similar it sounded like a chorus: 'Because it doesn't sell.'

THE SUPERMARKET

I asked consumers what is their understanding of a supermarket. To most, a supermarket is any self-service outlet.

There are supermarkets that fit this description such as Maponya's in Soweto and Khulani in Bisho. Supermarkets are perceived to offer better prices than general dealers or spazas. In rural markets and with the lower-end consumers in the townships, the bigger supermarkets compete strongly with chain supermarkets such as Pick 'n Pay, Shoprite, Spar, etc.

In urban areas, however, chain stores have the upper hand. But, I must stress, some black supermarkets do hold their ground.

In rural and peri-urban areas, local supermarkets are distributors with a Herculean muscle. In Bisho in the Eastern Cape a local supermarket, Khulani, had a brawl with a major international soft-drink supplier who treated them in the old South African way. They gave Khulani fridges like they did to all other major retailers. But because Khulani was 'black' they were expected to be more grateful because they got more than crumbs. 'Your brothers in the rest of Africa are worse off' is the usual argument.

When they complained about broken fridges, the drink supplier wouldn't take them seriously. Eventually Khulani told them to fetch their fridges, which they did. Everyone sat back to watch the big, black supermarket die of thirst.

Determined to survive, Khulani went to a smaller supplier that had been wanting to break into the market. Contrary to popular belief, consumers didn't stop buying cold-drink from Khulani. And the empties made a good 'traditional' weapon! The new cold-drink locked the drinkers to Khulani and their new supplier. Local stores also started stocking the new supplier's brands.

Realising that they would soon lose their jobs, the regional managers of the major supplier went back to Khulani. This was the owner's reply: 'Gentlemen, you're like a wife who deserted her husband, only to come back after he had married another woman . . .'

The moral of the story is that regional suppliers have to be extra-careful when dealing with local supermarkets, because supermarkets hold the key to their market. As Mr. Mabuna, a supermarket owner, said: 'We don't determine what people buy. But we have influence over their decision. Our goodwill is better than that of individual brands.'

Like a child nurtured in the backyard of bullies, Khulani

knows how to stand up to bullying suppliers, as was the case when they had another brawl, this time with a regional bakery. The bakery had been their trusted supplier for years, until they decided to try and cut them out by setting up an outlet in competition. They brought in their trucks and sold directly to Khulani's customers at a lower price. One of the managers at Khulani is reported to have said '*adakwa ngumbuso lamabhunu. Sizokuwabonisa*'. (These boers are power-drunk. We'll show them.)

To succeed, regional and local suppliers have to make allies with supermarkets and other traders.

Negotiations only brought acrimony. Left to their own devices, Khulani started their own bakery. They had one strength – they could supply bread that was hot from the oven. Their friend-turned-foe couldn't because they were in town while Khulani was in the township near its customers.

The bakery wanted to renegotiate but it was too late. They had pulled the noose themselves. I never made it to the funeral.

THE SPAZA SUPERMARKET

This is an 'imitation' supermarket – a convenience supermarket. It is also attached to someone's house but is bigger than the spaza and carries more stock. What makes it a supermarket is the self-service aspect. Consumers can walk through the aisles and choose their favourite products or brands without any assistance.

The aisles are small, leaving little room for point-of-sale material. Yet your brands need it if they are to gather attention instead of dust. The phrase 'it's not size that counts' has never been more relevant, especially among blacks. Here small things are required. But they must be able to make giants out of your brands.

THE STREET VENDORS

Street vendors who sell FMCGs are largely supported by impulse buyers. Some brands have already captured this market. At a taxi rank, bus or train station, or soccer stadium you're sure to find Simba Chips, Coca-Cola, boerewors rolls, etc. At some stations up to half a million people commute every day. On average a match between Orlando Pirates and Kaizer Chiefs attracts about 80 000 people.

Street vendors are like political commissars in a revolution. They are on the ground with supplies when the people need them most. I was introduced to several new brands of snacks at soccer stadiums or while waiting for the taxi to fill up. I have tried ice-cold drinks which were brought to the window of the taxi on a hot summer's day and I have seen many more people do the same. I have also seen many marketers pay no attention at all to this retail outlet. Pity.

MARKETING CONSIDERATIONS

- There are four channels of Fast Moving Consumer Goods (FMCGs): the general dealer, supermarket, spaza shop (and its variations) and the street vendor.
- Wholesalers play a crucial part in supplying the township trade.
- Marketers must establish a good relationship with the trade. Manufacturers should be careful not to market their own products or brands in competition with the trade.
- Only fast-movers are stocked by the trade.

9

In the townships it's not always hi-tech – it's hi-sense. There are no forklifts so workers have learnt to climb up these crates as if they form a staircase.

Chapter 9

BRANDS AND LESSONS FROM THE LIQUOR INDUSTRY

The difference between a product and a brand is the difference between *Homo sapiens* and Muhammad Ali. The former is generic and has no character. Brands have personality. They help define people. A BMW driver is different from an Audi driver.

Brands define a consumer's personality. What you drink tells others whether you've got money, style or character.

Even product categories define our status. The liquor category is a good example. The lowest on the social ladder is sorghum beer, which is perceived to be consumed by the down-and-out and is given the worst names such as *takunyisa,* which means 'will make you shit'. However, it is always brewed at traditional ceremonies. On the opposite end is J&B, which has been given the nickname 'Jabulani Bafana' which means 'Be happy, boys'.

Alcoholic drinks are not only about quenching thirst or getting tipsy. Most people I spoke to admitted that it tastes foul to the rookie. So why do they stomach it until they're used to the taste? I made it a point to ask all my respondents this question in liquor focus groups and in taverns. The answer was unequivocal – drinking is about belonging. 'I never used to drink, I started at college . . . the guys gave me the stuff. I had to drink it to become one of them,' said one respondent.

But belonging is not enough. The kind of group to which you belong counts even more. And liquor seems to define that grouping eloquently. It indicates whether you've got money, style or character.

'Savanna Dry says I'm young and I've got style,' according to Thami, a 19-year-old. 'Beer is for old-fashioned people,' his girlfriend said. They both enjoy 'gangsta rap' and their favourite lyrics include 'bitches' and 'niggers'.

On the other extreme is Cebo, a long-time drinker and an ardent supporter of Kaizer Chiefs, who claimed that he wouldn't be caught dead drinking Savanna Dry.

One day I organised a blind taste and invited him to participate. All my respondents were committed non-cider drinkers. I told them that this was a new drink, and wanted to see how it would be received in the market. The result was positive. They all thought it stood a chance and would buy it. Can you imagine their surprise when they discovered that it was a well-known cider? I wasn't. I had seen it in many groups. It's always the same.

In the past, women who drank beer and 'hot-stuff' were often regarded as 'indecent' and in some circles as cheap, even by other women. Cider became the long-awaited deliverer. When I questioned female respondents about drinking in public they told me very confidently: 'Yes, but this is a cider and not a beer. When people see me drinking this they know that I'm decent.'

THE ROLE OF THE SALES TEAM

A good sales force is a necessity if your product is to succeed in this category. South African Breweries has one of the most motivated sales forces in the country, and the leadership of their products bears testimony to this.

The sales team is the face of the marketer to the consumers. They build the brand by forming personal relationships with the trade and the local consumers. Drinkers interact with them at taverns and almost without reservation judge a brand by the people who market it. Reps also play an important role in the formation of a brand's character. They must play their part well, in everything from manner of dress to mode of transport. I've seen balding men trying to attract twenty-year-olds. Nothing looks sillier and it looks as though they are misleading the youth to drink.

Butiki, a taverner, told that he thought the mode of transport is very important: 'Reps get beautiful cars to make a good impression. The problem is that my tavern is situated in a place where there are pot-holes and it's muddy and dusty. I mean it's a normal township. Now the reps are reluctant to punish their sedans to come and see me. Now I must leave my tavern to go and see their stock here whereas they should be coming to me so I can continue with my business.

'Most reps do a sterling job, but man I don't know where they get some of them from,' said another taverner I spoke to. 'You can see that the guy is well educated but is not street smart at all. The problem is that reps are interviewed in an office environment and the human resources people want to see how they fit in the office as opposed to the streets where he'll be marketing the product.'

When speaking to reps I discovered that few wanted to spend time on new products or on reviving dying ones. The best way to move a product is to get the reps excited about it. This requires intensive internal marketing. Once that is achieved, it becomes easy for them to excite the consumer.

MARKETING CONSIDERATIONS

- Brands define the consumer's personality.
- In the case of liquor, it's the perceived image of a brand rather than the quality or taste of that brand that determines who will buy it.
- Reps build the brand by forming personal relationships with the trade and the local consumers. Reps should never be out of character with the brand.

10

In the spaza shop. Note the washing powders stocked – Omo and Surf. These are the brands that are known and that can be asked for by name.

Chapter 10

GETTING YOUR BRAND ON THAT CROWDED SHOPPING LIST

Picture this scenario: You are a family of seven with only two working adults. You don't have a car and most of the family members are under the age of 16. How would you do your monthly shopping? And what would you put on your shopping list?

Most consumers go through the process of making shopping lists and they inevitably have to make several trade-offs. The primary consideration is the universality of product usage – 'How many people can use this product at home?' The secondary consideration is manpower – 'How will I carry all these groceries from the shop to the taxi rank? And from the taxi to the house?'

Although most people earn on a monthly basis, there are still many who earn on a weekly or fortnightly basis and shop accordingly.

The challenge is to make your brand jump all those hurdles to get on that shopping list. And the best way to make it to that list is to make it become a household name like their cute little son 'My Dombolo',[1] or their troublesome baby daughter Maotoana,[2] whom they can't throw away.

Your brand must be part of the family or, at the very least, a family friend. It must touch their lives so they can put money aside for it at the end of the month. It must visit them frequently with its advertising because all good family members keep in touch. And most of all it must have its own idiosyncrasies like that bubbly aunt who is liked for her quirky humour or for her unmatched warmth.

A good brand is like a good friend. It understands your circumstances and is willing to adapt.

Lion Matches has done this very successfully over the years. Most people in the townships use Lion matches. They use them to light candles, stoves, pipes . . . the list is endless. Lion matches are as much a part of the family as of the individual. Lighting a candle is a family thing, but lighting a cigarette is an individual thing. The brand is built on a strong premise: 'As long as you've got a Lion, you've got a friend, friend.' It doesn't matter whether you're a young woman lighting a coal stove or an old man lighting a pipe, 'As long as you've got a Lion, you've got a friend, friend.' Over the years they've used-1

many different ways to demonstrate this and as a result they find themselves on many shopping lists.

A good family member or friend also knows the circumstances of the family, and adapts himself or herself to them.

Unilever knew that most families in the townships didn't have hot running water. Omo sold the fact that 'it works even in cold water'. I can still 'hear' those old radio advertisements in my head where the woman says '*Ngisho nasemanzini abandayo*' ('even in cold water').

They knew that back then getting hot water in the townships was a hassle. You had to make a fire in a stove or primer stove, put the kettle on and wait. Omo behaved like a good family member by promising good results even in humble 'pondokkie' conditions.

Some families keep live chickens, and those that can't, buy them. However, the increasing cost of chickens and other meats are putting them out of reach of the lower end of the market, which is still the biggest. These products are increasingly being sold by street vendors. Some buy their own cattle, sheep or goats, slaughter them and sell the meat. And if you want it grilled, you can get it there and then. The same occurs with milk and sour milk. Some milk distributors sell the milk directly to these vendors. Also, many people don't have fridges. So they buy items such as chicken, fish and red meat as and when they need them.

There has been much research on low-fat products and other first-world foods, but little on third-world foods such as a margarine that doesn't need refrigeration. There is a bigger market for those in the whole of Africa.

MARKETING CONSIDERATIONS

- Many people earn on a weekly or fortnightly basis, and their shopping patterns are shaped accordingly.
- There are many hurdles in the way of a marketer, from availability of transport to the lack of facilities. Marketers must make sure that their products enjoy top-of-mind awareness.

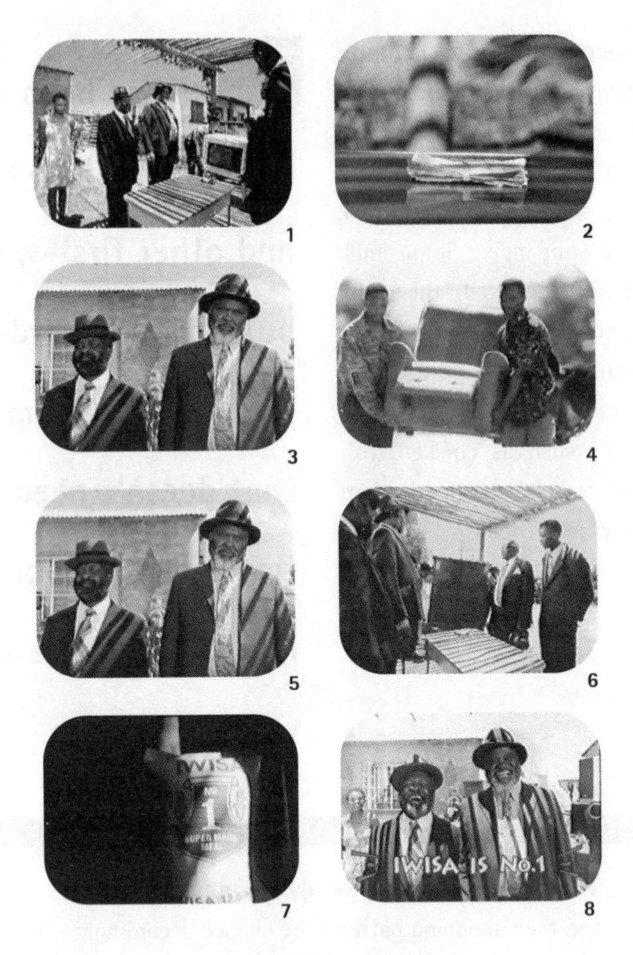

The lobolo ad that bombed.

MUSIC:

A popular black musician Tshepo Tshola.

THE STORY OF THE COMMERCIAL:

We see two elderly men (the bridal party) and the bride-to-be in the background.

NARRATOR:

In Africa the price of love is determined by the father of the bride . . . Fortunately, a wise woman knows that only the taste of Iwisa can melt a heart of stone.

[The groom's party brings money and puts it on the table. The bridal party refuses. The groom's party tries again. This time with a TV set. This is also refused. They try again. This time with a chair. This is also refused. Then the bride-to-be whispers something in a child's ear. The groom's party brings a bag of Iwisa maize meal. The bridal party nods and smiles.]

Chapter 11

PREPARING THE ADVERTISING (STRATEGY)

Your life may revolve around the product you are marketing or advertising. It may be the only thing you live for, particularly if the success of your company is measured against the success of your product in the market. You may even be very passionate about it. The rest of us, however, are too engrossed in our own problems to care. If you want us to be interested in your product, you must be interested in us. Know our traditions, know our lifestyle, know our dos and don'ts, and know our sensitivities.

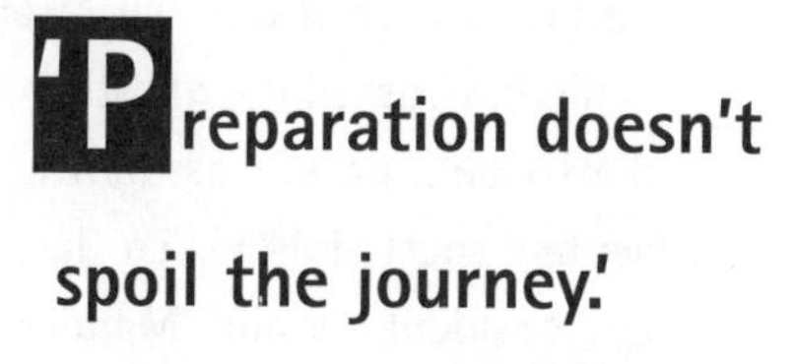
'Preparation doesn't spoil the journey.'
– African proverb

Iwisa Maize Meal is one of South Africa's leading brands in the black market. The advertising agency at the time, Hunt Lascaris, produced an ad based on *lobolo*. The ad shows a black family coming to pay *lobolo* for a girl. Money is offered but it's not enough. A wardrobe is offered, but it's still not enough. Eventually the bride's family is offered a sack of Iwisa and they agree to that. Can you believe it? Ten rand for *ilobolo*!

That ad offended Iwisa consumers. Hunt Lascaris lost the account. It was supposed to be funny. But it was probably funny only to the white agency. They never thought that it could be insulting to the people who eat Iwisa. If the people who wrote and produced the ad had the slightest interest in the lives of their target audience, they would have avoided such an insult. And the agency would probably still be handling the account.

Fortunately, the brand had already established a good relationship with black South Africans. It sponsored Kaizer Chiefs, one of South Africa's premier soccer teams, for a period of 21 years. It also established and sponsored Iwisa Spectacular, a charity soccer tournament, for 14 years raising more than 11 million rand in charity. Iwisa's relationship with the community was too strong to be ruined by an agency hungry for creative awards. Instead, it was the agency's relationship with the brand that was terminated.

INTEREST LEADS TO OPPORTUNITIES

By spending time with consumers both Old Mutual and *The Sowetan* discovered one of the things that is important to their market – nation building. When the idea to sponsor the Nation Builder of the Year Award was presented to them, they could have asked the question 'How will that help us sell more newspapers or life assurance?'. But that would have been acutely short-sighted. To date the award has been attended by President Nelson Mandela and other leading national figures. What better endorsement could you get?

IT PAYS TO LISTEN TO YOUR AUDIENCE

It is said that 99 per cent of communication is listening. How do you explain that in marketing terms? Quite simple. It means the marketer and the advertising agency should spend 99 per cent of their time listening to their target audience. They know more about their lives and needs than marketers or agencies ever will. Not this book nor any other similar ones nor the most comprehensive research can ever tell you more about your consumers' lives than themselves. So make it a habit of striking up a conversation with them, and do most of the listening.

Listening helped André Lubbe, a shoe-manufacturer, to sell thousands of pairs of Omega shoes in the black market. I visited him at his office once in Stellenbosch from where he runs his family business. He told me that once he was on holiday with his partner and he saw a young black boy wearing Omega shoes. He asked the boy about his shoes. Proud of his purchase, the boy went on like a slot machine. He told André that he walked long distances and these shoes were light, plus they had style. Bingo! Most blacks at that time didn't own cars and therefore walked longer distances than their white counterparts. There was the selling point for Omega shoes. Light and stylish.

Spend your time listening to your target audience. They'll listen to you if you listen to them.

André also markets a boot called Trailbusters. It's hugely successful in the white market. It is heavier than the Omega and is more functional than stylish. For now he is not even trying to market it in the townships because he knows that it won't succeed there. His consumers have told him so. And he is prepared to wait. My kind of man.

KNOW WHAT YOU'RE SELLING

I've always been amazed by copywriters who know very little about their products. If you read some ads, you can tell that the copywriter rewrote the brief and did nothing more. That is usually a result of laziness, and (let's spread the blame a bit) a difficult client. However, more often than not, it is the result of the copywriter's lack of knowledge about the particular product.

Advertising agencies have a high turnover of staff. So, when a copywriter or art director leaves the agency, they leave with product knowledge. This is the nature of the industry, and trying to change it would be like trying to change the landscape of the country.

As a client, if you're introduced to a new agency person you must make sure that he or she builds a good product knowledge by learning the history of the brand. That may sound tedious and the new person in the business may think you're being unreasonable. But then it goes with the territory. If he or she is reluctant to learn, you've got the wrong person on the account. Ask for a new person, or move your business.

BE OPEN-MINDED

Penicillin was discovered by accident. And that accident brought Alexander Fleming fame and fortune. Imagine what accidents can do for you?

This is marketing, not love. Consumers won't always love you the way you are. If you doubt that, ask Volkswagen and Nissan. When minibuses started replacing sedans as taxis in the townships, Volkswagen already had the minibus, the cult VW Kombi. Yet, unlike Nissan and Toyota, Volkswagen failed to capitalise on it and capture the booming market. Nissan launched the E-20 and Toyota relaunched the Hiace. At first both the E-20 and the Hiace were 10-seaters just like the VW Kombi. But some clever marketer realised that taxi-owners needed 15-seaters – I remember how I used to hate 15-seaters because they took longer to get full.

I liked Mr Khoza's taxi because it was a VW Microbus. And like his car manufacturer, he remained faithful to the original idea of using only 10-seaters. Unfortunately Mr Khoza went out of business, and almost every taxi is a 15-seater now. As for me, I've become accustomed to the waiting, which comes in handy when my 1968 Wolseley decides to break. My Wolseley? Mh! It breaks my heart. It is the reason why I'm always broke.

MARKETING CONSIDERATIONS

- As a rule, if you don't listen to your consumers, don't expect them to listen to you.
- It is important that agency staff really know the product they're marketing.
- Be open-minded about change and new opportunities.

12

Being young is about being carefree. Find out what your product is about, and concentrate on that.

Chapter 12

A LESSON FROM THE YOUNG: YFM

It happens. You have a big dream and no money to make it come true, or if you do have the money, it's just enough to make you taste your dream, only to watch it die.

YFM, a Gauteng radio station, was almost in a similar position. Y stands for Youth. Derek Hartford, a director at YFM, said to me: 'We had less than a third of what our competitors had. We could not afford to do classical marketing research. We had no money. We went and did our own research, we went to technikons and universities and invited students to come to our jols at lunch-time . . . We did it very unprofessionally. We played them music for about two hours, and they told us what exactly they were into. After that we had it clear in our minds the music they wanted.'

The signs are there for all to see. Use them.

Great marketers. No thick research reports, no complicated mathematical equations and no complicated theories.

'We could not afford any famous radio personalities and most of our guys had no previous radio experience. We had to train them,' Derek said. And like doctors sometimes do to their 'terminally ill' patients, experts told them that if YFM had no famous people on their station, they would be dead within a few months. 'Even record companies didn't have faith,' Derek told me; 'they refused to give us CDs to play on air.'

When YFM went on air for the first time, they had nothing but unknown DJs with CDs borrowed from their friends. Eighteen months later, contrary to the experts' predictions, YFM became the biggest regional radio station in the country with just under a million listeners. YFM has even brought us new names.

You'll never achieve success if you live by the rules set by your competitors.

'The signs were there for all to see, Muzi,' Derek told me. When he said that, I wished I could unscrew his head from the neck up and take it to marketers around the country so he can tell them, 'The signs are there for all to see. Use them, for goodness sake!' After that road-show I would return his thoughtful head to its deserving owner and say, 'Thank you, Derek. I hope they'll see the signs.'

The YFM philosophy was simple: Start a radio station that would cater to the interests of the black youth. The established radio stations (including black stations) weren't doing it the right way, even though they thought they were. According to Derek, when YFM started, 'some radio stations had even vowed never to play Kwaito!'[1]

There's only one thing behind YFM's success – doing simple things well. YFM entertains the youth, and they do it well.

I've attended some of their parties. They're always bursting at the seams. It takes a long time to get in, and seeing the 'stability unit' or riot squad is not unusual – they are there to control the crowds, because YFM listeners are prepared to die for their station. It's not that black youth is generally riotous, far from it. It is brand loyalty. YFM has turned the radio into a home for the fun-loving youth.

To achieve that they had to break every rule in the book, including the language barrier. Firstly, they do not confine themselves to the a particular language. Callers are welcome no matter which of the eleven languages the choose to speak. YFM even seems to have a twelfth language – 'tsotsi taal'. This makes the listeners feel at home.

THE PROBLEM WITH SERVING TWO MASTERS

Your target market is your master. They pay your bills. If you serve them well, you will go places in life. No one seems to understand that better than YFM. They strive to make their audience happy. If others become unhappy in the process then it is their own indaba.

One of YFM's bashes was attended by a government minister. At that time one of the popular songs was entitled 'I'm horny'. A YFM DJ who was also master of ceremonies shouted that he was horny, and wanted the audience to repeat after him. A journalist who was clearly not part of the target audience felt offended and slated YFM in the papers.

I listened to the programme as callers phoned in responding to the newspaper article. Listeners were not offended in the least. After-all, neither the minister nor the journalist was the target audience. Herein lies a lesson: if a company tries to be all things to all people it ends up being nothing to no one.

MARKETING CONSIDERATIONS

- The YFM success story indicates that there are many opportunities that conventional marketing cannot capture.
- You'll never achieve success if you live by the rules set by your competitors.
- You can never serve more that one master in marketing.

13

A product with a witty name – and it's been number one for a long time.

Chapter 13

NAMING THE PRODUCT

According to Cathleen Airey, an official at the Registry of Trademarks, there were 25 720 applications in 1998 for new trademarks, all seeking the attention of consumers. These will not only fight it out among themselves but will have to try and unseat the already existing trademarks of products and services.

Trying to unseat a market leader is like trying to unseat a Third World dictator – it is hard and costly. History is full of corporate martyrs who died trying. You need a powerful name to do so.

Trying to unseat a market leader is like trying to unseat a Third World dictator – it is hard and costly.

Unilever knows what I'm talking about. They launched a black hair product and called it Esteem. The market leader at the time was Black-Like-Me. Unilever had far more money and management expertise than Black-Like-Me. Still, Esteem failed. I couldn't establish the exact amount of money lost but I know somebody who saw truck-loads of the product being driven away to be dumped.

I'm glad Unilever was big enough to cut its losses. Most marketers wouldn't. They'd rather hang in there and hope that someday their luck will change. 'After all', a young black brand manager once told me, 'marketing is a struggle, it took 350 years for a black person to eventually lead South Africa.'

It is easier to have a memorable name if your brand is the first in its category. Colgate means toothpaste to many people because it was the first in South Africa. All my childhood I grew up knowing that 'groovy' meant any can of cold-drink. As a child I used to go to the store and ask for a 'Groovy Coke'. It was only in 1999 that I discovered that Groovy was the first cold-drink to be produced in cans.

Simba Chips was the first in the black market, and is still the market leader by far. It never occurred to me until much later in life that Simba was a brand *and* company name. For a long time 'Simba Chips' meant any cold chips in a packet of 25g or more.

One of my most embarrassing moments occurred in my first few months at Ogilvy & Mather when I said to the Willard's client, 'Are Willards Simba chips crunchier?' If only words could be taken back, and if only that floor at O&M could open so I could disappear. Fortunately, he didn't throw a tantrum. 'Yes, Willard's chips are crunchier than Simba,' he replied.

A successful product will attract competitors like moths to a flame. Choose a name that will outlive its founders and hold its established position in the minds of consumers.

A category cannot remain new forever. A successful product attracts competitors like moths to a flame. In most instances the competition has more money and better technology. Black-Like-Me attracted Carson and Procter & Gamble.

When naming a product, choose a name that will last because good brands outlive their founders. When it was launched, the name Black-Like-Me was apt in the context of prevailing black consciousness. When was the last time you heard people shout 'black power'? This, coupled with lack of brand building on the side of Black-Like-Me, led to Black-Like-Me losing its position to Dark & Lovely. The latter has connotations of both blackness and beauty.

Names that denote average quality should be avoided like the plague. A name like OK Bazaars was doomed to fail on two counts. Firstly, a product with a 'name and surname' is cumbersome and sooner or later people will shorten it. In the case of OK Bazaars people dropped Bazaars and called it OK. A shop called OK can never be seen to be selling quality products. What it sells is nothing more than okay. Nothing special. Compare this with Shoprite, which conveys 'shopping right'. No wonder Shoprite swallowed OK. Shoprite is a kind of name that will stand for a long time, all things being equal. It has meaning.

Another example of a marketing blunder; this time by the venerable Pick 'n Pay group. They have a subsidiary called Rite-value. This may look good in the short term because the company will steal from the equity of Shoprite, and therefore save the company on advertising. However, in the long term that name will mean nothing more than a second-rate shop that is first among the unoriginal. The suffix 'rite' has become a property of Shoprite. Legal minds may not think so but consumers do. And that's all that matters.

A brand with a witty name stands the greatest chance of succeeding in the market. Iwisa Maize Meal is a good example. People use maize meal to make pap, which is a gut filler. 'Iwisa' is a Zulu word for a big, beautiful knobkerrie. '*Iwisa liyayiwisa indlala*' people used to say and that means 'Iwisa knocks starvation down'. There you go. Iwisa is the market leader by far.

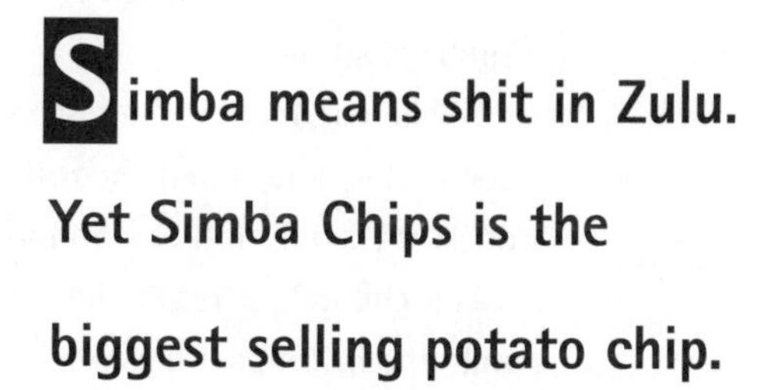

Simba means shit in Zulu.
Yet Simba Chips is the
biggest selling potato chip.

When a name is presented to the marketer it is usually presented on beautifully mounted boards. Marketers and their agencies tend to forget that the product will be advertised on radio where no one will see its spelling. Also, word of mouth is one of the best endorsements a product can get. They may talk about it at home, on the bus, at a public toilet, tavern or anywhere else where they may not have the product with them. So, the name of your product should be memorable and easy to pronounce.

Despite the above traps, being the first can let you get away with anything. The best example is provided by Simba Chips. 'Simba' is Swahili for lion. But in Zulu 'simba' means shit. And there are far more Zulu speakers in this country than Swahili speakers.

'*Unama*simba *wena*' rude people sometimes say, meaning 'you're full of shit'. '*Susa ama*simba *omntwana*', that's what soccer fans shout when the fullback kicks the ball away from the eighteen-yard area, and it means 'remove the child's shit'. (A child's shit can be used for witchcraft.) And the most frequently uttered line in factory floors is '*unama*simba *lomlungu*' – 'this white man is full of shit'.

Mothers always say '*ngiphethe ama*simba *chips*', which means 'I've got simba chips'. (People can't see your respectful capital letters when you talk.) Yet the Simba brand is the strongest potato-chip brand in the country. I know this because I once conducted consumer research for a rival brand. Simba is strong.

While conducting the research I asked spoke to some users about this, and asked them if it ever bothered them. 'Yes, it does,' replied a mother who has been enjoying them since she was a child. As a result she substitutes the 'S' with a 'Z' and calls them Zimba Chips. As for the majority of consumers? Does it bother them? No. They simply don't associate snacks with shit. Yet Simba is successful because it was first in the market.

MARKETING CONSIDERATIONS

- The name of your product must be memorable and easy to pronounce.
- If you want your product to flourish, avoid names that connote mediocrity.
- Choose a name that will not be restricted to a particular era or trend.
- Be careful of clever names and remember that consumers won't always see the spelling of your product's name.
- Being first in a category is the best position to be in.

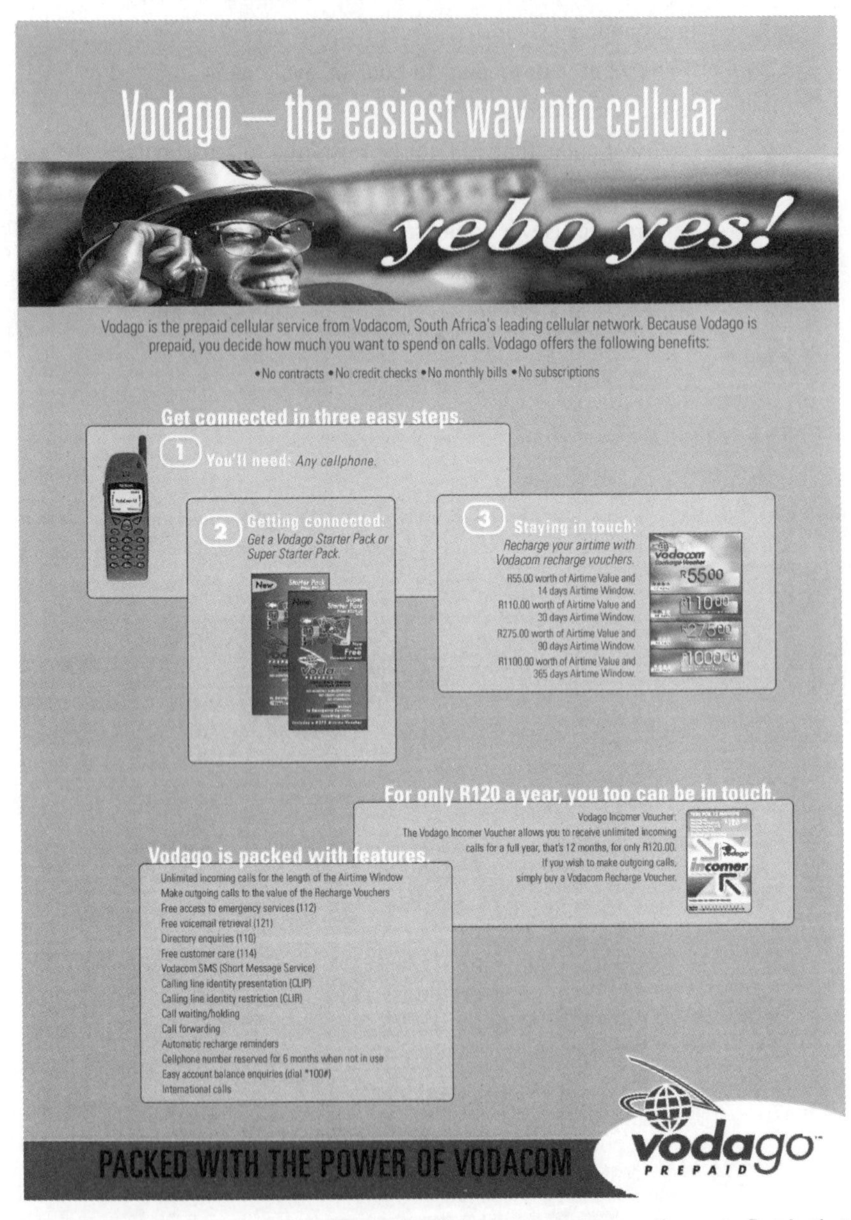

Vodacom and MTN were bound to succeed in cellular telephony because they were first in that category. It will take a big marketing blunder for either company to lose substantial market share to new entrants into the industry.

Don and Thandi Thankge on their wedding day.

< Street vendors are like political commissars in a revolution – they are on the ground with supplies when the people need them most.

As part of nation-building, many young people used murals to decorate the townships. Savvy marketers moved quickly. >

TOWARDS THE FUTURE

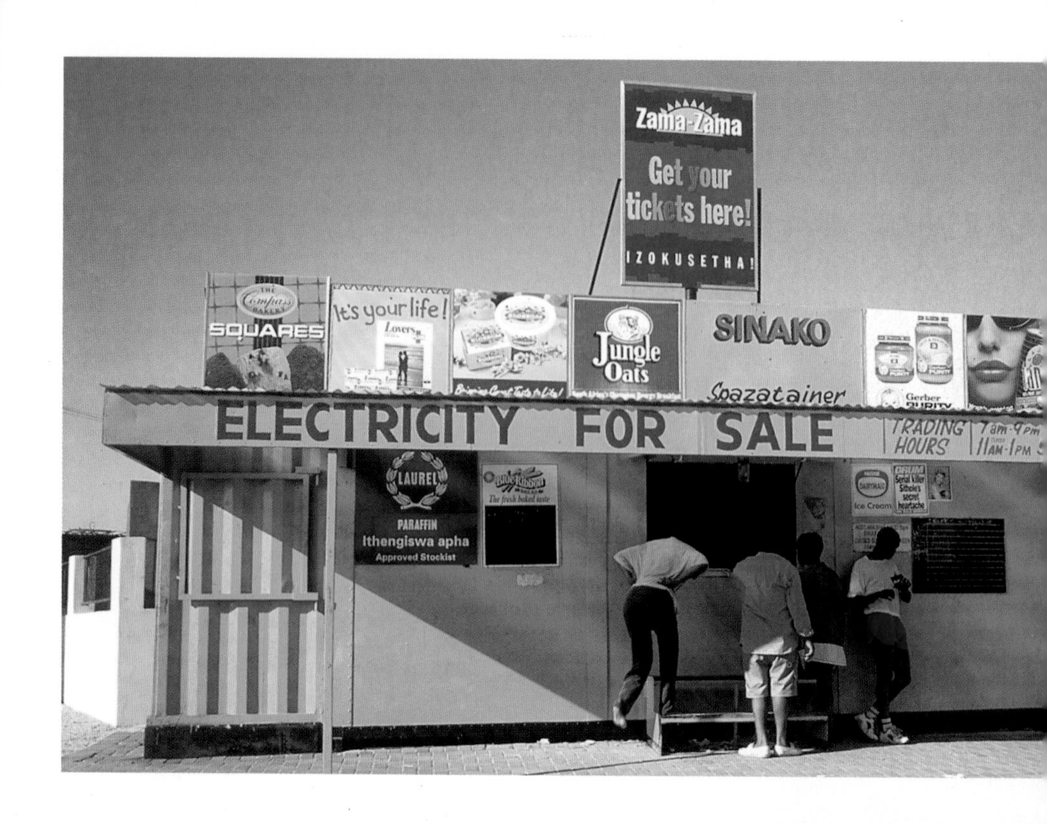

A colourful township tavern. Some taverns are more than just channels of distribution – visiting them conveys an important message about who you are. >

< A township spaza – the convenient convenience store. Service at these shops is over the counter so it helps if consumers know your product name.

COR

Although an ad showing a black Father Christmas may be interesting to whites,
to blacks a black Father Christmas is as common as a navel.
To the black consumer this Father Christmas is made no more special by being black.

TO BE A WORLD FAMOUS TAXI YOU HAVE TO OUT RUN THE COMPETITION

Like the London Taxi in England and the Yellow Cab in America, the Toyota Hi-Ace has endeared itself to millions of South Africans because only the strongest survive the harsh conditions that vehicles are subjected to in the taxi industry. For over 20 years the Toyota Hi-Ace has faithfully carried the nation in comfort and in style. It is called the Zola Budd by those who appreciate its superb performance. It has been crowned the people's carrier by those who swear by its reliability. It is simply the "High Ace" to those who know it's the best and the toughest in the business.

Its legendary 2,2/Toyota 4Y engine, a powerhouse capable of unleashing 75kW at 5200r/min, is mated to a smooth 5-speed transmission. Take the improved all-round suspension as well as the rack and pinion steering, you've got a vehicle that will keep your business going right. With a host of standard features, the Toyota Hi-Ace Super-T is custom-designed for the taxi industry • central locking • reinforced side step • improved remote control immobiliser.

Backed by over 300 dedicated Toyota dealers countrywide, you can rely on the Toyota Hi-Ace to never let you down. **Everything keeps going right**

TOYOTA

H I - A C E

Toyota captured the lion's share of the mini-bus taxi market in South Africa by listening to taxi drivers and owners, and consequently by changing their product to suit local conditions.

Chapter 14

LAUNCHING A NEW BRAND

A product stands the greatest chance of succeeding if it starts a new category. It becomes the foundation of the category by becoming its generic name. Simba Chips was the first and is still the market leader in its category. Colgate is generic for toothpaste to many people. The list goes on.

It's not always possible to launch a new category. In that case it is better to find a niche within the category, and concentrate on it. As the saying goes, 'there are riches in niches'.

Stellenbosch Farmers Winery launched a product called Savanna Dry. Black consumers in all my research groups classified it as a cider, but it was a unique colour in a unique bottle. They fell in love with it. They talked about it and saw it more at stokvels, street bashes, parties, beaches than on the media. For a long time, Savanna was both talk of the town and the in thing to drink.

Consumers are increasingly becoming wise to the tricks of the marketing world.

Using celebrities to launch a product works if the particular product is in their area of expertise. For instance, it makes sense for a famous soccer star to endorse a pair of soccer boots or energy products. Jomo Sono, the king of soccer, has a soccer boot named after him, 'Puma Jomo Sono'. It has been on the market for years and is doing well. Do you think the Jomo Sono brand would work if it had been extended to jeans and shirts? I doubt it. Doctor '16V' Khumalo had a clothing label named after him. It was called 16V. At first it sold well. But within a short period of time there was no trace of the label in stores. Furthermore, celebrities are expensive and their credibility can be questionable.

Celebrities are in the public eye. When they falter, the public is quick to know about it. And that affects your brand.

Mzwakhe Mbuli, the famous people's poet, was endorsing Metrorail when he was arrested for a bank robbery. The commercials were changed. Months after he had been convicted, I was watching a soccer game on television with a group of guys. When a new Metrorail commercial came on, one of the guys asked, 'Shame. I wonder how Mzwakhe is doing in prison?'

Consumers are discovering the tricks of the marketing world. They know that people are paid to endorse products. Some celebrities endorse too many products to be credible.

Ordinary people with character launch brands better. They are believable. Fresca, a cold-drink, was launched using Hakeem Kae-Kazim, who was virtually unknown in South Africa at the time. Omo uses ordinary housewives. Old Mutual uses ordinary policy-holders. YFM launched with no famous DJs and still beat the star-studded Kaya FM. These advertisements work because they are credible. Ordinary people add the most important thing to your brand-credibility.

MARKETING CONSIDERATIONS

- A product stands the greatest chance of succeeding if it starts a new category or creates the perception of a new category.
- Launching a product with a celebrity no longer works as well as it used to. Most celebrities endorse too many products to be credible.
- Many products have been launched successfully without the astronomical fees of celebrities.

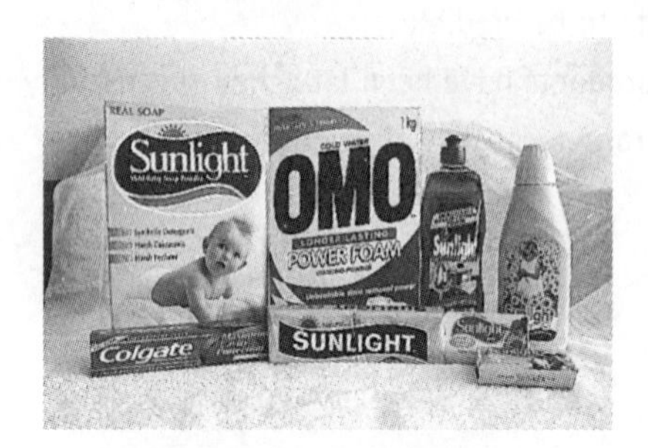

Colgate and Omo are not as extended as Sunlight, and have acquired generic status. Sunlight, although long established, has not achieved the same generic status in most black households.

Chapter 15

BRAND EXTENSIONS

At 25 my hormones started pumping and I became broody. I started thinking about the number of children I'd like to have and their possible names. I dreamt of having three children: Muzi Kawande Kuzwayo, Muzi Uyanda Kuzwayo, Muzi Wandile Kuzwayo. These names have meaning. The first one means 'let the household of Kuzwayo grow', the second one 'the household of Kuzwayo is growing' and the third one means 'the household of Kuzwayo has grown'. It's crazy, isn't it? But that's what brand extensions do to products. Most of them are crazy.

In the short term brand extensions may increase sales. But in the long term they'll harm the core brand.

Omo is the market leader in the washing powder category. Wouldn't it make sense to extend the brand to Omo fabric softener, Omo bleach and Omo all-things-to-do-with-washing? That is not the view at Unilever, and that's great. In the short term, extending their brand would increase sales, but in the long term it would harm Unilever's greatest asset – the brand.

Surf, which is Unilever's number two, is also not extended. It is a soap powder and nothing else. Sunlight, which is one of Unilever's most extended brands, is not as successful. You get Sunlight soap, Sunlight fabric softener, Sunlight dishwasher. Neither Sunlight soap nor its fabric softener is the market leader in its category. Unilever can afford Sunlight just to keep competitors out of the market. However, its dishwashing liquid is one of the top brands because it was one of the first in the market.

It is easy to be tempted to extend your brand. Many people used to take Bob Martins dog pills because they believed that the pills helped their hair grow. I confess with a bit of embarrassment that there was a packet at home even though we've never owned a dog. It belonged to my aunt. Her friends also had packets of Bob Martins. And they didn't have dogs either.

I phoned Martin & Martin Pharmaceuticals, the manufacturer of Bob Martins, and I was put through to Bridgitte Fitschen. I asked her if she knew about people taking their dog pills for themselves. 'Yes,' was her reply. 'We find a lot of people asking us if these products can harm them. We tell them that they have been made for animals.'

'If that is the case, why didn't you launch a multivitamin targeted at the humans considering that you already have a market?' I asked her.

'Because the animal brand would lose its credibility,' she replied.

Great marketers!

If your company has already launched a brand extension, it is never too late to mend. Mike Mhlongo, a product manager at Bromor Foods at the time, once gave me a brown packet of Cadbury's. It wasn't chocolate but an instant mash potato called Cadbury's Smash. Cadbury means chocolate. It was not the first time that I saw a Cadbury brand extension. There are Cadbury chocolate sweets. During my school days they were the biggest sellers. Cadbury chocolate sweets had a successful advertising campaign that is still vivid in my mind – a precocious school boy asks his teacher, 'Sir, how do Cadbury's put chocolate into the sweet?'

'How they put it in is not important. What is important is how you take it out,' the teacher replies.

Each time I looked at that packet of mash potato I asked myself, 'How do Cadbury add chocolate into their potatoes?' The thought of chocolate mash potato was hard to swallow. It took me more than six months to open that packet. Even then it was because it was mid-winter, mid-month and I was broke. I had to eat it. I think, given a choice I would have thrown it away.

To Cadbury's eternal credit, Cadbury's Smash was repackaged and relaunched simply as Smash under the Bromor Foods label. The new pack is mouth-watering indeed, which goes to show that it's never too late to change; look and change direction as soon as you realise you're wrong. When I spoke to Zanele Ngubane, the brand manager, she said, 'We realised that the name Cadbury, strong as it is, won't add any value to Smash, because Cadbury is synonymous with chocolate.'

Cadbury-Schweppes has become a good example of a company that does not believe in senseless brand extensions. They own two subsidiaries, namely Cadbury (Pty) Ltd and Bromor Foods (Pty) Ltd. The brand names under which they market their products in various categories include Cadbury's (chocolates), Schweppes (mixers), Lemon Twist (cold-drink), Chappies (chewing gum), Energade (sports drink) and Moirs (jelly and custard).

MARKETING CONSIDERATIONS

- Brand extensions can harm the core brand.
- If you have to extend into different categories, use different brand names.
- It's never too late to 'undo' unsuccessful brand extensions but implement change as soon as it becomes apparent that your brand extensions are not getting off the ground.

Ms. RATLHOGO:
It is a right for every person to be educated. It is not a privilege. Whe my son, Mpho, was born, it was hard. I was teaching till late afternoon. Then when he was in Standard One, I taught him to play chess. It was then that I realised that he is somehow talented. Then started saving money specifically sc that when he passed Standard Ten there should be some money waiting for him. Mpho is now studying Mechanical Engineering i Cape Town University. It means as parent I have succeeded in bringin up a responsible adult-to-be.

She invested R50 a month for 10 years

We'd like to help you make the most
of your life, every step of the way.
OLD MUTUAL

Old Mutual built its campaign around 'helping people making the most of their lives', and demonstrated this by providing examples of clients who benefited from going to Old Mutual.

Chapter 16

BRAND BUILDING

In the past it took some time to build a brand. It took years to build Coca-Cola, Snowflake, IBM and many others. However, media technology has greatly reduced that building period. Dimension Data, Ixchange, DKNY and Tommy Hilfiger are a few brand names that became big within a short period of time.

Some managers tend to become arrogant when their brands become successful. I've heard many marketers saying: 'Our brand is now famous. We don't need to advertise anymore.'

But once a brand has been built, it must be maintained through advertising and other forms of communication. This is how Dark & Lovely overtook Black-Like-Me. Black-Like-Me never had a brand-building advertising campaign until it was too late.

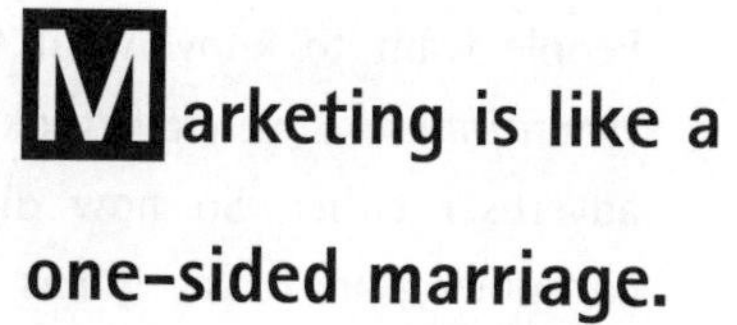
Marketing is like a one-sided marriage.

It's to remember that your consumers aren't your employees – they don't care. Marketing is like a one-sided marriage. Only one party has to make it work and that is the marketer.

The communications industry is always fighting over whether or not the budget should be allocated for above-the-line or below-the-line communication. Above-the-line advertising is conventional advertising and is more glamorous than its lesser siblings, namely promotions, public relations, etc. The fence-sitters always say they believe in 'through-the-line' advertising so they can make money on both sides.

The truth is that both forms of communication have their place. In non-urban communities, for instance, print media have little penetration because of high levels of illiteracy. Some homes do not own television sets and many of those that do have black and white sets which do not accurately show the colours of products.

When I was in Standard 3 in a Bantu education school, I could not read well. We did not have a television set at home. We had a radio which, like all other radios, could not show the product. So how did Colgate make sure that I knew about their product? They sent 'Mother Colgate'. She came to our primary school and taught us how to brush our teeth. She did that in many schools. It may sound patronising, but if you think about it, how many working parents have time to teach their children how to brush their teeth?

Brand building no longer means putting a commercial in the media and expecting that people will buy your product. People want to know what the product can do for them. When Dark & Lovely overtook Black-Like-Me it was no great advertiser either. So how did they do it? Educating the consumer. Dark & Lovely has a hair academy and an army of technicians who travel around the world looking at new black hairstyles. Hair salons around the country are invited to see new trends and products.

But it does not end there: the technicians go to various hair salons both in town and in the townships to teach hairstylists how to create the new hairstyles. This attracts clients to the hair salon and it reinforces the relationship between the salon and Carson's (the owner of the Dark & Lovely brand).

To keep that relationship warm, Carson's organises a competition between salons and the winner is sent to the Broner ethnic hair show in Atlanta, USA. What could be better than that?

Iwisa Maize Meal became even bigger than it already was ,by sponsoring Iwisa Kaizer Chiefs. As an adman I was heart-broken when I heard that Iwisa Maize Meal, the biggest mealie meal brand, was to stop sponsoring what was then called Iwisa Kaizer Chiefs Football Club. I declare my loyalties upfront – I am an Orlando Pirates fan, and these guys are our arch-rivals.

For those who like numbers, each team in the Premier division plays 34 games. Each game is 90 minutes long. That is 3060 minutes of free advertising per year. Granted, not every game is televised but that figure excludes the number of radio stations that broadcast football matches, newspaper reports and commentary, as well as competition games. Iwisa, on the other hand, did help Chiefs with badly needed money at the time. It was sad to see the two part ways. But as the marketing manager of Iwisa, Ian Bennet, said, 'It had become too expensive. Kaizer Chiefs had become an international team and the investment for Iwisa couldn't justify the return, especially for maize meal.' What can I say? Some relationships aren't meant to last forever.

Toyota virtually owns the taxi market in South Africa. Surprisingly, they were not the first in that market. Speak to Mr Joe Speelman and you will see that great brand builders are mostly down-to-earth, hard-working people. Toyota realised long ago that the economic future of this country lies with blacks. And whoever dominated that market would be the richest.

At first black taxis were largely American sedans. When American car manufacturers left the country because of apartheid, the Nissan E-20 became the popular taxi. At the time both Toyota and Volkswagen had light commercial vehicles. In the township the Toyota was called '*Nkatjibane*', in other areas it was called '*Inkom' ephuza amanzi*' ('the cow that only drinks water') because it was considered to be light on petrol. The VW was called the *Khumbi,* from the popular SA term 'Kombi'.

But Nissan became the market leader for a while. Toyota regrouped and came up with a plan that would change the market for a long time to come. At first they made sure that their product was suitable for township roads, which require a 4x4 at best or a military vehicle at worst. They relaunched the Toyota Hiace, and constantly researched the durability of their product. This research did not only occur at their manufacturing plant; they also spoke to taxi owners, taxi associations and passengers to find out about both the real and perceived problems.

They discovered that there was a problem with the rear door – it broke easily. The sliding door used to go off the railings and the side step used to crack. They sent the car to Japan to be improved, and also to look at the peculiar South African tradition of stop and start. (Have you ever wondered how many times a taxi stops and starts in town? It's worse in the townships.) That investment finally paid off. They had the best product for the South African taxi industry.

Price is relevant but so is quality in determining the long-term success of a strong brand.

At the core of every strong brand is a quality product. Especially in Africa. Carson markets its products throughout the continent. And their financial director, Alvin Nadas, agrees: 'If you have a quality brand in Africa and good distribution you're on your way to success. Price is the issue but not the only issue.'

Price is last on the marketing commandments. As one woman I spoke to said: 'Price does not matter, because if it did, poor people would stop buying expensive clothes, alcohol and cigarettes.' Nissan tried to fight the taxi war on price and sold its E-20 for less. Toyota mobilised the taxi owners further. The company kept a closer relationship with the taxi mother bodies. They sponsored their conferences when everyone else thought it beneath them. They also built a conference centre for them.

Toyota started training the taxi owners about how to run the taxi business. They outsourced this to a company of white consultants who couldn't speak the same language as the taxi drivers. Mr Speelman was promoted to a management position and he went to the heart of the problem – language. He was right. Why should one pay people who only speak English to train people who are mostly illiterate and cannot understand the language?

Bra Joe changed the content and format of the training. He visited various universities and technikons looking for ways to teach the uneducated masses of South Africa. He couldn't find one because they are by their very nature for the élite, the educated. He eventually found a solution after attending a International Labour Organisation course. He realised that he needed to use imagery more than text.

In 1998 alone Toyota trained 720 taxi owners on how to run the taxi business. Included were 91 widows whose husbands had died during taxi violence and who were left with the taxis and no one to run them.

What was the result of all this? The market pioneer, the Nissan E-20, is now dead. And of the 3317 new 16-seaters sold in 1997, 2943 were Toyotas. Who can argue with an 89% share of sales?

In places like Pretoria, the VW Bus is making a comeback as a used car. I spoke to several taxi owners about why they prefer the VW Bus. 'It's more spacious,' and 'As a second-hand car it is cheaper than the Toyota,' some said. On investigating further, I was told that most of them run on Toyota engines. 'What?' I exclaimed. 'Yes. Many used VW Microbus bodies powered by Toyota engines.' I asked a few township mechanics about this. Bra Matsotsana, a mechanic, summed up what all of them said in long-winded ways: 'If you want to be rich, you must buy a Toyota. It is the only car that obeys its master. It knows that you buy it to serve you, and not the other way round. It's reliable, cheaper to maintain and it can go long distances, which is why people call it the Zola Budd.'

I've met many people who think that above-the-line advertising is the corner-stone of the brand building process. I disagree. Advertising is only the visible exterior of the building that both the consumers and competitors see. Within the building are equally important components and in marketing terms these are quality, reliability, and below-the-line communication.

MARKETING CONSIDERATIONS

- Brand building is no longer as time-consuming as in the past. It's now possible to build a successful brand within a couple of years.
- Brand building requires more than above-the-line advertising. Do not undervalue the impact of below-the-line communication in the black market.
- Blacks at management level are not only necessary for political reasons, but for new brand building and other marketing ideas as well.
- Brand building requires more than above-the-line advertising. It requires establishing a good relationship with the trade.

Volkswagen abandoned a powerful brand position: 'People's cars'.

MUSIC:
All employees of Volkswagen from the Managing Director to the shop-floor staff are singing in the choir. The tune is of the people of South Africa. There is a mixture of western instruments and an African beat.
LYRICS:
VW and me, we all believe in quality, you're our kind of people in the Volkswagen family.
TITLES:
Isn't that what you'd expect from Volkswagen?

Chapter 17

POSITIONING THE BRAND

Who was William Shakespeare? A playwright. Who was Martin Luther King Jr? A civil rights leader. Both these men did several other things in their lifetimes, yet we describe both of them in a few words.

The same is true for products. Budget car rental means just that, inexpensive car rentals. No one else can own that position in the mind of the consumer. Toyota means reliability. BMW means luxury. And Nissan? In many people's eyes it doesn't stand for anything because it hasn't been consistent. In the last few years they have changed their positioning several times. A few years ago it was 'We are driven.' Then it changed to 'You can with a Nissan', now it is 'Life is a journey. Enjoy the ride.' Compare that to Toyota's consistent 'Everything keeps going right'. It has remained unchanged over the years. Is it any wonder that the Nissan E-20 went out of production? Volkswagen had a slogan 'Isn't that what you'd expect from Volkswagen?' but they forgot to demonstrate *what* it is that we should expect from them. Volkswagen had a strong position which they should never have abandoned: 'People's Cars.' People's cars are reliable and inexpensive. When VW changed that positioning, Toyota took it. And today it outsells VW. The perception exists that Toyota is cheaper and more economical but in reality it is not. At the time of writing this an entry level VW Citi Golf 1300 sold for R41 490 while an entry level Toyota Tazz sold for R45 909. The Golf has five gears and the Toyota has four. A Toyota needs to be serviced every 10 000 kilometres and a VW every 15 000. So which is more economical? VW or Toyota? No question, the VW. But what do most consumers think? Toyota.

VW continues to bring woes onto itself. A few years ago it launched the GTi, which was dubbed the 'legend'. That was fine. The people can have a legend. After all Nelson Mandela is a legend. But when VW launched the Golf VR6 it eroded the GTi's legendary status. The GTi could no longer claim to be the legend. And now the Golf VR6 has been dropped from the Golf IV range. The GTi is left to fight it alone without its bigger brother. Can it reclaim its legendary position of the 1980s? I don't know. But one thing is for sure: if someone comes with his VR6, he can tell me to go to hell with my smaller GTi IV with a 1.8 engine. What can I say? As Mongezi put it: 'Girls prefer the guy who drives a VR6.'

Similo has owned two BMWs as well as a 4x4. Before buying his first one, he considered the VR6. Then he looked at the price tag and found that he could get a BMW for the same price. 'I thought I might as well get a more prestigious car than a VW,' he said. 'Jetta is also in the same price range. And this is why a lot of black managers moved to BMWs. The Jetta was a middle manager's car. But that has changed.'

For brand positioning to be effective, it must be consistent.

If VW had to introduce a performance car like the VR6, they should have introduced it under a new brand name and definitely not as a people's car. That would have been costly but at least the VW brand would have remained what it was – reliable, inexpensive and outselling Toyota.

Lack of consistency is not peculiar to Nissan or VW. Toyota is now doing it too. 'Welcome to our world' is what some of the ads and brochures say. If no one puts a stop to such inconsistency soon, erosion will start. No one noticed Edgars eroding its brand with its famous ultra-cheap red hanger sale. It happens every year. What message did that send to people? 'Edgars is ridiculously expensive. Come and buy only when the red hanger sale is on.' It's not a consumer who told me this, but several Edgars' employees. No wonder the company's earnings dropped in 1999. Fortunately for shareholders, Edgars quickly changed management and the company is bouncing back fast.

Brand erosion is like rock erosion – no one notices it until the damage is done.

For international brands positioning has become critical especially with international media such as CNN and satellite television beaming into our lounges. Again, consistency is likely to be affected.

In South Africa, BMW is associated with 'sheer driving pleasure' whereas in many overseas countries it is associated with 'the ultimate driving machine'. After paying hundreds of thousands of rands I want pleasure. Not a factory machine. I am not being biased towards my countrymen [or is it country-person?] but Hunt Lascaris came up with the best line.

With international media exposure we are starting to see the German version of 'Freude am Fahren', as if that means anything to people like Mbhazima Shilowa (Premier of Gauteng) or Jacob Zuma (Deputy President of South Africa). To them, as it probably does to many South Africans who've done well with little education, it probably sounds like 'Vorsprung durch Technik'. I guess we might as well start saying 'Auf Wiedersehen' to the BMW brand unless something is done about the uniformity and consistency of its message worldwide.

MARKETING CONSIDERATIONS

- Brand positioning must be simple.
- For brand positioning to be effective, it must be consistent.
- International media such as satellite television are sending conflicting messages about brands. Companies must find solutions to these soon.

18

So, what's unusual about a black Father Christmas?

Chapter 18

THE DIRTY CLINIC SYNDROME – WEAK POSITIONING

The reason why some brands fail is because of weak positioning. A hospital that positions itself as clean won't attract any patients because a hospital is expected to be clean. Only if it is dirty will people talk. So, when positioning a product you must go beyond the expected.

Many black empowerment companies fell victim to this in the early days of the empowerment process. All they offered their partners was the fact that they are black. Politically that may have been a good thing because it aimed at redressing past imbalances, and may have helped the company to win a few government tenders, but from a marketing point of view it is grossly insufficient.

In heaven an angel is no one special. In South Africa, a black person is no one special.

National Sorghum Breweries (NSB) launched a clear beer called Eyethu. If you read the press statements before the launch, you would have thought that the end of South African Breweries was nigh. The reason why NSB failed was because Eyethu was poorly positioned. The ads said 'Iyavaya. Eyethu' – 'It's nice. It's ours'. How did blacks respond? The brand never made a dent on SAB's market. Instead NSB lost money and what was supposed to be a black empowerment company ended up belonging to the Malaysians. This goes to show that people won't drink a beer just because it is brewed by blacks. As the saying goes, in heaven an angel is no one special. In South Africa, a black person is no one special.

NSB should have targeted a particular segment of the beer-drinking market instead of trying to capture the whole market. But it is common in marketing to try to appeal to everyone, especially with mass-market products like beer. So next time someone says 'We'll take the whole market', remind them that even Nelson Mandela, the most popular name of our time, never appealed to everyone.

Many clients have come to me wanting to launch new products. 'How does your product differ from the competition?' I've asked. 'Ours is a quality product. It is better than the competition because it's got features a, b and c.' Consumers don't buy the quality angle, especially with high-end products. If you pay a lot of money for a product, you expect it to be quality.

The quality of products is similar to the cleanliness of a hospital. Quality is the core of a good product, but people don't buy fruit to eat the core. They want the sweet part. 'Sheer Driving Pleasure' say the BMW ads, not 'Sheer Quality'.

Many black media owners complain that they do not have much advertising support as they should. From December 1997 to December 1998 black newspapers and magazines received R223.5 million in advertising, and the white media or mainstream newspapers received R1764.9 million.[1] I spoke to several media planners and directors about this situation.

'There are various reasons for this,' said a media director who asked not to be named. 'Most media planners are young, white yuppies and mostly women with little or no knowledge of the black market or media. We have to change the make-up of planning departments. The industry must train black media planners.' I had a feeling that he was being politically correct with me. After all, he is a media person, he'll know all the politically correct buzzwords. But I was wrong. He continued to tell me a truth which I would have liked to hide from white people. Unfortunately, I am a non-fiction writer. And non-fiction writers must be truthful. And truth does not change because it is told by a person of a different colour.

'Many people are too idle or disinterested to get into the media industry. They are not willing to do their rounds and to develop a good understanding of media, even though we have a fast-tracking process in place. If black media owners can provide excellent service, a good product and the discipline to sell their product in agencies, they will thrive. Look at the biggest media player in South Africa, the SABC,' the media director said. And I knew what to expect. 'Who owns the SABC?' he asked.

'It's the government,' I replied.

'And what is the colour of the government?' he pressed on.

'Black,' I admitted.

'And the SABC Action Stations (African languages) are the best run stations in the country. Their product is great, their service is great and they market their services well,' he said.

'What a breath of fresh air,' I thought.

'The fact that a person is black, Muzi,' said Nyakale Mokgosi passionately, 'is a cherry on top. But if the cake is not well baked, nobody will buy it. Look at Kaya FM.[2] They are supposed to be a black radio station targeting affluent blacks. But they have few listeners. Blacks won't listen to you just because you're black. Your programming must be right. And your advertising must be correct.'

MARKETING CONSIDERATIONS

- No 3-year-old has ever bought a sweet simply because the manufacturer is 30 per cent black-owned. This is true for any product for any target market.
- Consumers expect premium products to be quality. So, quality alone is a weak position.

HERDBUOYS McCANN-ERICKSON SOUTH AFRICA

REACHER MARKET
TIMBALAND / AFRICAN RETRO

Rap.

I played basketball on a court in the Bronx
where they say hip-hop was born/
and kicked raps till dawn
Lamajita know that I lay the law/
I told them mzansi tales of/ peace and war
Then in the west/ batshwere style sa bona and/
From Japan to Puerto Rico it's on/
But I dropped mega songs lyrically/ in street psalms
And I thought, do all these overseas places
Mean that the African races
Sit in second place?
It looks like/ wena and I
Sikhipha ama verse that can split the sky
In the 99
Think don't blink
If I don't be my African self
I'm gonna sink.

Trust your instincts
Obey your thirst
Sprite.

357 Rivonia Boulevard, Sandton, 2128. P.O. Box 10663, Johannesburg, 2000 Phone (011) 235-4600 Fax (011) 803-4222

Directors: Les Broude, Quintin Denyssen, Clive Haines (British), Carol Keenan, Alan McClarty, Happy Ntshingila, Simon Rowcliffe (British), Steve Richards (British), Dimape Serenyane, Yolanda Tomlinson, B. Peter Vundla, Brian Watson (British)

(Proprietary) Limited. A McCann-Erickson Worldwide Company. Reg. No. 97/02258/07

Sprite changed the international image of its campain to suit the South African market.

Chapter 19

CHANGING THE BRAND AND ITS POSITIONING

There are times when a brand has to change its name. Thank goodness we have moved on from the days when the government used to ban newspapers and force publishers to change their brands. An example of this is *The World,* which was banned and later changed to *The Post. The Post* was also banned and re-emerged as *The Sowetan.*

Some changes occur due to political changes. For instance, *Bantu World* changed to *The World* even before it was banned. Brands that bear old South African names such as Transvaal are better off changed. This kind of change does not harm the brand. In fact resisting it could. If Namibian Breweries was still called the South West African Breweries, Windhoek Lager would probably not sell in this country. Any product called Rhodesian whatever would certainly go the way of Rhodesia.

When Mr Brian van Rooyen (who is black) launched his consulting company he didn't use his name, as is the trend in most cases. He looked at the times. 'I couldn't call it Van Rooyen and Associates post-1994, the name Van Rooyen wouldn't have gone down too well.'[1]

Other brands change their names for more practical reasons. Datsun changed to Nissan because the company changed internationally. Indeed Datsun would have looked like an orphan while every other car manufacturer had an international mother company.

However, trying to change the brand by repositioning it to suit international trends can be dangerous. J&B Whisky abandoned a powerful position. 'True pleasure is rare,' said the ads. Now they say 'The brighter side of life'. This is dangerous. Whisky is a pleasure and it is scarcer than brandy or beer.

A commercial can't run forever, but the spirit of the campaign can. 'Everything keeps going right' has been running for ages. Unfortunately when agencies win accounts, they want to put their stamp on the brand and change it. Even if it means killing the original, winning concept. And as a developing nation, more often than not, we will be forced to execute other countries' strategies.

Herdbuoys McCann Erickson had the guts to change Sprite's international positioning to suit the South African market. Internationally Sprite commercials say 'Image is nothing. Thirst is everything'. When speaking to Kaibe Mollo and the then Client Service Director on the account, Rori Maclean, they said, 'The truth is that in South Africa image is everything. And to deny it would be dishonest. So the ads were changed to say, "Trust your instinct. Obey your thirst."'

The results speak for themselves: Herdbuoys was able to produce some of the highest-scoring advertisements in the country. Sprite's growth rate changed dramatically, with South Africa becoming the fastest-growing Sprite drinker in the world. (I was asked not to use the figures because of trade secrets.)

Sometimes it's difficult for a brand to find consumers in its chosen positioning. The consumers may have moved on, and the brand may have failed to attract new ones. The brand must then be moved up. The clothing chain Ackermans did that successfully. They were in the lower end of the market with depressing shops. They revamped their stores and advertising, which immediately elevated the brand.

Pages Stores, which was a clothing chain with 186 stores countrywide, was targeted at the lower-income black market. Things were tough there because that's where everyone wants to be. Moreover, Pages had become boring. The chain has been relaunched as Exact. It remains to be seen how Exact will do in its new market.

There is a saying that goes, 'Spend time with a saint and

you'll discover that his stool smells too.' As time passes, bad perceptions can develop about a brand.

I looked at two case studies to support this, namely Bertrams VO and Mainstay Cane Spirits. These brands were favourites when I grew up, the choice of township aristocrats.

Spend time with a saint and you'll discover that his stool smells too. As time passes, bad perceptions can develop about a brand.

But perceptions have changed. They are now associated with low-income heavy drinkers who couldn't afford decent spirits. 'What is the problem with these brands?' I asked consumers. 'This happens all the time,' some respondents from Rockville, Soweto, told me. 'When a product is first launched, it is the best. But as it becomes popular, the producers pay less attention to quality and more on volume.' This may not be the case but it is a perception that the consumers out there have and it must be dealt with.

Part of the brand-building exercise is to reassure consumers that you are true to the principles that made you succeed in the first place.

'We change with the times, I mean . . . how many times has BMW changed its shape in the last ten years? Do you want to tell me that if they had stuck to the same shape people would still be buying it?' That's how Mlungisi sees things. 'I want new things. I don't want to be drinking the same thing that my father used to drink. I mean, there's a 35-year difference between me and that guy. Drinking what he used to drinkwould mean I'm 35 years backwards.'

'But you *are* 35 years behind him,' I interjected.

'Biologically yes. But as far as technology and other things go, I'm not. In fact, I'm 35 years ahead of him.'

At Mlungisi's age don't we all think that we know better than our parents? And so deserve better?

But we shouldn't fool ourselves. Sometimes change is inevitable. And when changes are implemented they can never be painless no matter how gradual we try to make them. But unlike birth, which cannot be postponed forever, changing an image can be done. Postponing change is worse than postponing circumcision. Firstly the trauma becomes psychological. You start imagining the scissors and the knives that will cut you. Then you start asking yourself the 'what ifs' . . . 'what if the doctor cuts the . . . what if it doesn't heal . . .' And if you don't go through with it you will never be regarded as a grown-up man in some cultures.

SAB knows what I'm talking about. When their largest-selling brand, Castle Lager, changed its packaging, it lost many consumers. Consumers always reminded me of this case study in focus groups. They insisted that SAB had not only changed the packaging but the formula as well, that it had reneged on its promise of 'somewhat dry, somewhat bitter but never sweet', which was the then Castle Lager pay-off line. Consumers made all sorts of accusations, from sweet to weak. SAB, on the other hand, insisted that they hadn't changed the formula.

Nevertheless, sooner or later, the marketer will have to decide whether to do the painful operation now, suffer the traumatic postponement or let the brand die a slow death. Besides, at times consumers welcome change because it liberates them.

MARKETING CONSIDERATIONS

- Reasons for changing a brand name

1. New political dispensation.
2. International associations.
3. To suit the South African marketing environment.
4. Consumers have moved on.
5. The brand has developed bad connotations.

- Change the appearance of a brand before the market thinks it is outdated.
- Do not change the brand or its positioning just because you have appointed a new agency.
- When your brand undergoes change, you're likely to lose many consumers, which means losing market share. But as soon as those consumers realise that your 'new, improved' brand is not poisonous, they're more than likely to come back.

20

Oros	**National Brands**
Royco	**Bromor Foods**
Cerebos	**Unifoods**
Koo	**Robertsons**
Knorr	**Langeberg**

Can you connect the brand with the correct company?

Chapter 20

THE BRAND NAME VERSUS THE COMPANY NAME

I asked several women who use Dark & Lovely if they knew any of Carson's products. Many of them didn't. Carson manufactures Dark & Lovely. Many people who bought Oros at a supermarket didn't know Bromor Foods, ardent users of Royco soup didn't know Unifoods, and those who bought Cerebos salt didn't know National Brands, and some with Koo products didn't know Langeberg.

Some marketers, however, always insist that the company name should also be made into a brand. In most instances there is no need to advertise the company name. It only confuses the consumers, and sometimes it can turn them off. I approached several consumers who buy at Stuttafords, an upmarket department store: 'Do you know that Pepkor owns Stuttafords?'

In the minds of most consumers, the brand name is the company name.

'What? That company that owns cheap stuff near the stations? I can't believe it.'

South African Breweries is one of few companies that are as well known as their individual brands. SAB is a virtual monopoly anyway. The problem with consumers knowing your product as well as the brand name is that when they are fed up with the company they will shun all your products. This is one of the reasons why Windhoek Lager became so successful. 'It provides a fresh escape from the monolithic SAB,' Mubango, a Windhoek Lager drinker, told me.

Bromor Foods owns the number one and two orange squash brands, namely Oros and Brookes respectively. Unilever owns Omo and Surf, also number one and two respectively. The company name is good for traders, and for investors at the stock exchange, but not for the consumer.

In the minds of most consumers, the brand name is the company name. Knorr is both the company and brand, and Cream of Mushroom and Cream of Tomato are the flavours. What most consumers don't care to know is that Robertson's manufactures the products. Consumers trust a Knorr or Royco product. And advertisers should take the view of consumers.

The same kind of thinking extends to bigger brands. People see the Corolla as a flavour in the grand Toyota brand. So is the Camry. The E-20 was a flavour of the Nissan brand and company. The Golf is a flavour of the VW brand and company. Consumers see a car that comes from Toyota as reliable and inexpensive to run. If they feel money is no longer an issue, they'll probably buy a Lexus.

MARKETING CONSIDERATIONS

- The company name should be used for the benefit of the trade and the investment community, and not consumers.
- If a company's brand portfolio extends to many categories, advertising the company name can have the same effect as brand extension – it can be disastrous for other brands.

SECTION III
CLEARING OUT THE COBWEBS

IT'S TIME THE CORPORATE LADDER FELL.
Don't miss this year's National Conference, AGM, and Black Manager of the Year Award to be held at one of the most beautiful place in the world, Cape Town.
For more details contact Ms Siobhan McCarthy at KOPANANG CONFERENCE CO-ORDINATOR Tel. (021) 439-5933 or 083 301 7010. Fax. (021) 439-5153.
BMF
Restoring our dignity throug transformative empowerme

The day this commercial ran in the newspapers, the first people who responded were white males who complained that the ad was fascist!

Chapter 21

DOES ADVERTISING WORK?

'May I speak to your Chief Executive please?' I pleaded with the woman on the other side of the phone.

'Mr Jack is busy. Would you like to leave a message?'

Since running my own business, I've learnt that the high and the mighty never return the calls of lesser mortals like us.

'Okay, I would like to speak to him about handling your advertising account, ma'am,' I replied.

'Please send Mr Jack a fax detailing what you want. He'll return your call as soon as he gets a chance,' she replied.

I faxed Mr Jack. No less than two minutes after sending the fax, even before thinking about the next prospect, my cell-phone rang.

'Bill Jack here from African Life. I am returning your call,' said a Scottish-sounding voice.

It was like getting a call from the ancestors. I didn't know what to say. I must admit, I wasn't expecting Mr Jack to return my call. I expected him to act like a typical Chief Executive and not return calls.

'Advertising life assurance', Mr Jack said, 'is a waste of time and money.'

I liked that, not because I enjoy rejection but because I was about to make history – I was about to convert an adamant CE from being an absolute non-believer to a devout convert. 'Advertising works, Mr Jack,' I replied. 'Look at companies like Metropolitan Life, Old Mutual and Sanlam. They advertise,' I replied, trying to defend my profession.

'They are wasting their money. Life assurance is unlike soap. It is sold and not bought.'

I couldn't argue with Mr Jack. African Life was doing extremely well. There was no doubt that this man knew what he was doing, and obviously knew what he was talking about. I thanked him, feeling more like a boxer on the canvas than an ad man. 'It's a pleasure,' he replied and apologised for rejecting my proposal.

Mr Jack had a point. Some brands became big with little or no advertising at all. I knew about Microsoft's Windows '95 before I saw the advertisements. Dark & Lovely became the market leader in the black hair category with a very small advertising budget. Unilever, on the other hand, tried to enter that market with Esteem and put millions behind it, only to see it die. Windhoek Lager grew big with an insignificant budget compared to that of South African Breweries.

So why advertise? '*Ukuzala ukuzelula*' goes an African adage. Loosely translated it means having a child is extending one's reach. Incidentally, good brands behave like good children. When times are bad, they help the parent company to pull through, and when they are good, they help it excel. Think about it, how many recessions has Coca-Cola survived?

The English have a saying, 'Spare the rod and spoil the child'; in marketing the adage should say 'Spare the rand and spoil the brand'. Shun advertising and you shun market share.

An advertising budget is like a country's defence budget. Even Switzerland spent 4637 million Swiss francs on defence in 1998/9. And they haven't been to war in over seven hundred years. That is because they don't know when the next rogue will attack them. Black-Like-Me never knew when Carson was going to launch their attack. And when Carson did attack they found it easy to take the market.

Advertising makes it difficult for the competitors to enter your market. Coca-Cola's advertising budget has made it difficult for Pepsi to enter the market, although the latter helped Coca-Cola by following a suicidal formula – the directors earned high salaries and drove expensive cars. There is no problem with this as long as you aren't likely to get liquidated. But the brothers should have known that before you can enjoy the fruit, you must till the soil, water the tree, prune it and wait. Marketing is about patience.

Brand attacks may come from the least expected quarters, even non-competitors. When Schweppes introduced Dry Lemon, little did they know that they would hurt uncompetitive brands. When Dry Lemon was introduced, it became 'cool' to be seen drinking it. Brandies with which it could not be mixed fell by the wayside.

Before you can enjoy the fruit, you must till the soil, water the tree, prune it and wait. Marketing is about patience.

In certain categories like alcohol, consumers try new brands repeatedly. 'Finding the right drink is like finding Ms Right,' said one of the respondents; 'it's not an overnight thing.'

'What do you mean the right 'drink'?' I asked.

'I mean one that's good for you . . . one that doesn't treat you badly the following day,' he replied.

This 'how it treats me' is a very important in certain categories. It's all a matter of perception rather than reality. And a strong advertising presence assures an accurate and effective perception of the brand in the minds of consumers.

MARKETING CONSIDERATIONS

- Some brands have become big with no advertising at all.
- Advertising makes it difficult for your competitors to enter your market.
- Advertising makes it difficult for the competition to attract converts from your product.

22

A boring ad on a boring building – all part of a boring campaign.

Chapter 22

THE CAMPAIGN THAT FAILED – AIDS AWARENESS

It was a cold winter's night and I was watching women doing aerobics. I felt rather uncomfortable because I was looking through the window and any passers-by could have been forgiven for thinking that I was a peeping tom. But while I was still grappling with my guilty feelings, I noticed a middle-aged man peeping through the keyhole. I didn't want to be associated with *that* sort of lowliness. However, I needed to speak to the instructor to arrange an interview with her, which was why I was there in the first place. I decided I would go earlier the following day to catch her before class began.

As I walked away, the keyhole peeper followed me. He came right up to me, assuming that I was a comrade-in-peeping. 'These girls are playing with this thing while we want to kiss it,' he said. I thought I'd become accustomed to strangers saying embarrassing things to me because I always ask them about their personal lives. But this one caught me completely off-guard. I couldn't respond. Thank goodness he proceeded: 'But there is one thing that's killing us. HIV. AIDS is killing the nation.' Before he could finish this thought, he noticed a group of women going in the opposite direction. 'Hello, cherries,' he greeted. At first they looked at us with amazement, then laughed and greeted back. I couldn't tell whether they were laughing at us or whether they were just being polite. My hunch, however, was that they were laughing at us. That's a small price to pay

Social campaigns require accountability. Without it, lack of direction and apathy are inevitable.

for walking with strangers.

'I am good in bed,' he continued with his conversation. 'Once I sleep with a woman, she'll keep coming back. There is a married woman that I sleep with. She comes to me three or four times a week and asks me to sleep with her.'

I wanted to ask him if he took any precautions about AIDS seeing that he preached to me about it first. I couldn't find a polite way of asking him. I felt ashamed that at this day and age I could not ask people whether or not they used condoms. Realising that I had nothing to lose except an unplanned interview I asked him, 'So does she bring her own condoms?'

'No,' he replied.

'But how do you know if she doesn't sleep with other men besides you?' I asked him.

'She is still a virgin.'

'But she is married, isn't she?'

'Yes she is married, but she hasn't slept with her husband yet,' he replied. 'I can tell that they haven't slept together because she is still very tight. She cries each time I sleep with her. Plus it's easy to see someone who is HIV positive. They've got many pimples on their faces. If you see a woman who has many pimples, stay away,' he advised.

We got to the end of our road and we had to part ways. The keyhole peeper worried me. I asked myself how many other people had a similar view of AIDS. Equally worrying was the advice of one of the government officials responsible for AIDS education in the Department of Health. I phoned this official to enquire about what I should do to help educate people about AIDS. 'Muzi, my brother,' he replied, 'save yourself the trouble. People go on as if they own the disease. You would think that it was founded by their parents and it is part of their inheritance. No one should do anything about it in the media without consulting them. AIDS activists, politicians and journalists have made it impossible to work without fearing to upset someone in this campaign. You can't do decent work without offending at least one of the stake-holders.'

Still, he offered to look at my proposal. I thanked him but took his advice. I never sent it. What is sad is that while egos get in the way of the AIDS Awareness Campaign, people who know nothing about AIDS walk the streets.

The problem with the AIDS campaign is that no one has been held accountable. When Edgars Stores' earnings dropped they quickly put their account up for pitch. AIDS, unfortunately, has no client. Donors keep donating, the government keeps spending yet people keep contracting the virus. Shame, isn't it?

Poppie (not her real name) is an AIDS worker. She has no faith in the campaign. When I asked to talk to her about her work she referred me to their media liaison person. There I would get the official statement. But it is not the official statement that I'm interested in. It is the truth. As for Poppie, she does not believe that what she is doing will bear any fruit.

'What is the problem, Poppie?' I asked.

'The communication is wrong,' she replied. 'We produce all these brochures, yet the majority of our people are illiterate. The message is irrelevant. It is not real. There is a TV programme called Soul City. They use actors who we all know are not HIV positive. Soul City passes for great entertainment but not for reality, and AIDS is real,' she said heating up.

23

This commercial won big awards but failed to gain any market share for the product. The result? The product is no longer on the market.

A man and his wife are sleeping. He wakes up.
MAN: Alison, wake up.
WOMAN: Mh!
MAN: Darling, I'm making you some Aspro-clear.
WOMAN: What?
MAN: Aspro-clear. The new effervescent pain-killer. Because it's a fizzy it dissolves into a clear liquid.
WOMAN: Aspro-clear?
MAN: Yes, it's absorbed fast to relieve aches, pains, fever, headaches.
WOMAN: But Paul, I don't have a headache.
MAN: EXCELLENT!
MUSIC: Love making music in the background.
CUT TO: Pack shot and pay-off line: All you need is Aspro-clear.

Chapter 23

WHY SOME AD CAMPAIGNS ARE MORE SUCCESSFUL THAN OTHERS

It's a strange observation that the most successful campaigns have nothing to do with winning awards. In fact some award winners have been withdrawn from the market while some of the companies that produce them are doing badly. Awards such as the Loeries pride themselves on being judged by 'peers'. The problem with the 'peers' is that they are almost all white males who live in enviable riches; a completely different world from that of the rest of the population. '*Kulele kunye. Ngabe kubili, ngabe kuyavusana*' – 'They are together in their sleep. If there were two, they'd wake each other up.'

In advertising, market winners aren't necessarily award winners and vice versa.

Nando's has won many awards. But say that to shareholders and you'll probably be kicked in the teeth. The company's shares fell from a high of R1.80 in 1997 to 42 cents in December 1999.

'We opened some stores in the second half of last year that didn't quite perform the way we would have liked them to,'[1] said the chairman, Robbie Brozin. To solve their problems, they may franchise some of their stores as recommended by the US research companies they deal with. In my view, Nando's shouldn't be looking so far afield. The question they should be asking is, 'Does our advertising appeal to the masses that must come and buy our chicken instead of that of our competitors?' Clever plans from international business schools don't mean anything if consumers don't buy your products. Especially with a mass product like chicken.

Nando's is making a big push into the black market. They

have arranged with the Industrial Development Corporation to make finance available to black entrepreneurs. If it is to win the chicken war, it's must be funnier than S'dumo and Tiny of Chicken Licken. It is possible. The problem is that the judges at the Loeries might not understand the humour.

Aspro-clear, a pain-killer, also won several awards including the coveted Gold Lion at Cannes. It's no longer in the market. I asked the Head of the Consumer Division at Roche Pharmaceuticals, Alan Main, about the ad. 'Everybody liked the ad except the consumers,' he told me. Roche launched a new multivitamin brand called Superdyne. According to Bridgitte Fitschen of Martin & Martin Pharmaceuticals, the multivitamin category is a difficult one with heavy competition. Yet Roche was able to sell 100 per cent more than their expectations. Alan Main says the agency warned him not to expect any awards from the advertising campaign. His reply: 'I don't care how many awards a campaign *doesn't* win. As long as it brings me a return on my investment.'

No one ever goes to boxing match to watch the coaches box. Brands must compete, not agencies.

Shareholders (or the owners of the business) aren't investing to win awards. They want financial gain. No one practises that better than Edgars. A few days after they reported a serious drop in their earnings, they put their business up for pitch and appointed a new agency.

However, it should be remembered that the client–agency relationship is a difficult one. If CEOs on the clients' side do not increase shareholders' returns, they don't get salary increases or they get fired. If the creative people on the agency side don't win awards, they don't get salary increases and sometimes get fired.

I always tell marketers and advertising people that no one ever goes to a boxing match to watch the coaches box. It is the brands that must compete, and the coaches must be where they should be – in their corners.

Many successful advertising campaigns do not win glamorous awards. The 1999 ANC election campaign will never win awards, yet it helped win 66.38 per cent of the seats in parliament.

The co-founder of Ogilvy & Mather, Rightford, Searle-Tripp and Makin, Brian Searle-Tripp, used to say to me, 'We are in the business of building our clients' brands. If we do good work, then we will win awards.' He surely knows what he is talking about. His agency has won hundreds of local and international awards, and in 1995 he became the first person to win the South African Creative Directors' Forum Hall of Fame Award.

Unfortunately, most of us are in the business of winning awards; if they build clients' brands, great, and if they don't, tough.

MARKETING CONSIDERATIONS

- The fact that an ad wins awards does not necessarily mean that the product will be successful in the marketplace.
- At the same time, however, the complexity of the client–agency relationship should be kept in mind.

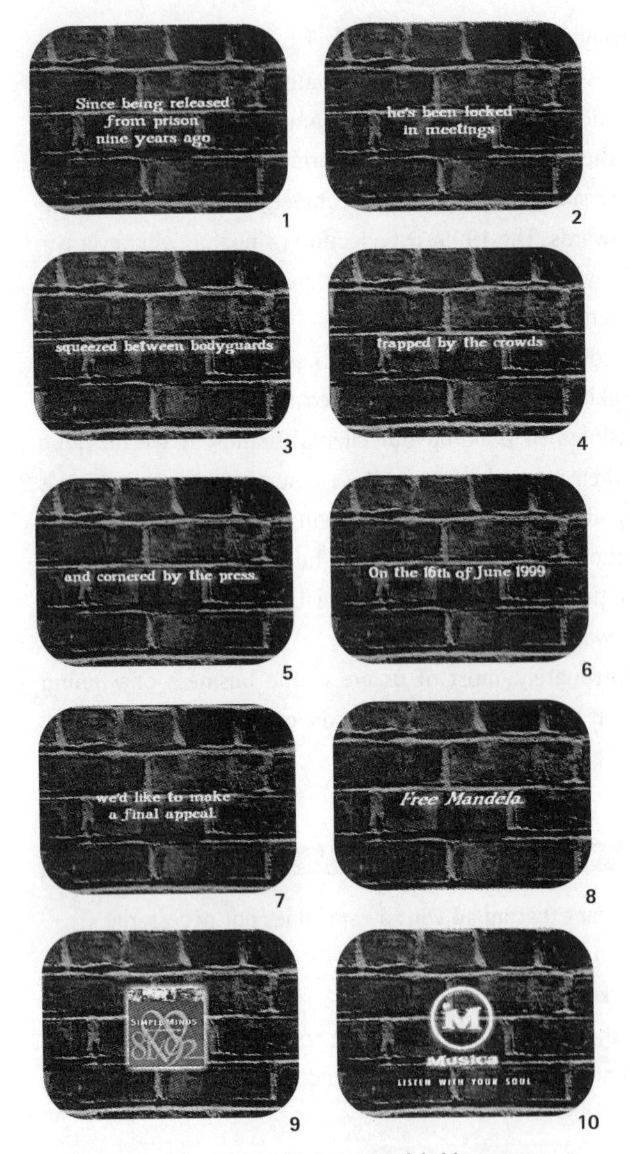

This is one of the best tactical commercials I have ever seen.

Chapter 24

CREATING GREAT ADVERTISING

Pretty pictures don't make companies great. Ideas do. Your latest typefaces, catchy jingles and glitzy commercials are all worth a bean if you don't know how to communicate.

But what is an idea? Mh! How do you explain love to a 10-year-old? Or *ubuntu*? It's one of those things which are difficult to define yet are conspicuous even by their absence. But for an idea to yield its intended benefits it must be relevant. And relevance is two-fold. First, there's relevance to your intended audience. Can they identify with your message? Does it move them? Or does it leave them cold? Or worse still, does it turn them away? I once saw an ad that poked fun at mothers-in-law. This may be thought of as humorous in the white community, but it's taboo in our community.

The second kind of relevance is that of the benefits or features the product. What's the point of powerful imagery and sounds if they are irrelevant to your selling message or product?

Stale ideas are like stale bread – neither sell in a free society.

If you're going to spend all that money on advertising and you have a brilliant idea, you had better make sure that your ad is seen and sells. The ad must have an impact. If it fails to achieve that, then it attempts to be what it's not – art. Advertising people are not artists, they are artisans.

Stale ideas are like stale bread – neither sell in a free society. Unfortunately the majority of ad ideas created for my community are now tired. Either they are produced by uninterested people or by grossly ignorant souls who won't deviate an inch from the teachings of their fossilised mentors. Next time you place an ad that Africans are going to see, hear or read, please make sure it is fresh.

Advertising masters say the best way to create an ad is by finding the critical fact of the product. And keep it simple – deletions improve, additions ruin.

An ad must make me believe that I will benefit from using the product. It must convince me. Not teach me. That might have worked while we were still forced to look up to the white face for direction. Now that we are free, ads must go beyond superlative descriptions of the product and recognise that I too can think as well as the person who wrote it.

A retired prostitute once said nothing is lower than a cheap client; one who takes what he wants and leaves without rewarding you. Many ads are guilty of that. Hundreds of ads burst into our homes every day, do their job and leave without entertaining or fascinating us. How cheeky! An ad must reward the viewer. It can be humorous, shocking, witty or charming but ultimately it must appeal to our emotions. Some ads are remembered for being spectacularly boring, others for being assertive in their stupidity. Both those are dangerous things to be remembered for.

Humour is probably one of the best selling tools. Don't we like people who make us laugh? Nando's does it well. But if you're going to use humour, please remember the first rule of humour: be funny. When I was a junior in an ad agency, I was commissioned to study African humour. It was a good idea, the problem is that laughter disappears when you start analysing it. One thing to remember is that South African blacks enjoy Hollywood as well as local comedy. But local is *lekkerder.* Think of TV programs like Living Single, and compare that to *Umuzi wezinsizwa.*

The only problem with humour is that it seems to be culturally divided. A black entertainer once said he watched the popular sitcom called Seinfeld but couldn't find the punch lines!

Some ads suck you in and raise your level of interest first.

When you're thoroughly involved and have forgotten that you're watching an ad, they deliver their selling message.

Self-deprecation is one of those rare human traits which can be endearing a great deal. Avis was able to create a great campaign by accepting that they were number two. 'We try harder' was their line. I hope that most of the clients who create ads targeted at us learn that there is more good than harm in not taking yourself too seriously.

Believability is equally important. It's difficult to say what makes one ad more believable than the next. There are some real hyperboles which consumers gladly accept and some middle-of-the-road honest-looking salesmen who don't make the cut. It all boils down to fascination. If you're fascinating you can get away with anything.

The features of your product are also important but they don't sell products – benefits do. If you want to find out what your product's benefits are, speak to consumers, sales staff, shop assistants or anyone who uses your product. Once I was looking for office furniture. After speaking to the saleswoman, I asked the cleaning lady which furniture was the best. She told me how difficult it was to clean certain types and how sensitive they were to things such as hot cups and stains. Things the saleswoman didn't know.

MARKETING CONSIDERATIONS

- Advertisements must be relevant to work.
- They should also, above all else, attract and reward the viewer by being humorous, by appealing to their emotions and by being interesting.

Slaat a jika in die toun or hit the long road, alles is sharp.

Hardly surprising when you consider that the Toyota Hi-Ace Super T was the first vehicle especially designed to meet the needs of the taxi industry. Sporting all the livery that sets it apart, the beauty of the Hi-Ace Super T is more than skin deep. Underneath lurks the legendary 2,2l Toyota 4Y engine. A powerhouse that is capable of unleashing 75kw at 5200 r/min. Add the new rack and pinion steering and the improved front and rear suspension, you've got a super taxi that responds to every command. With the backing of over 300 Toyota dealers countrywide, you can be sure that the Hi-Ace Super T will never let you down.

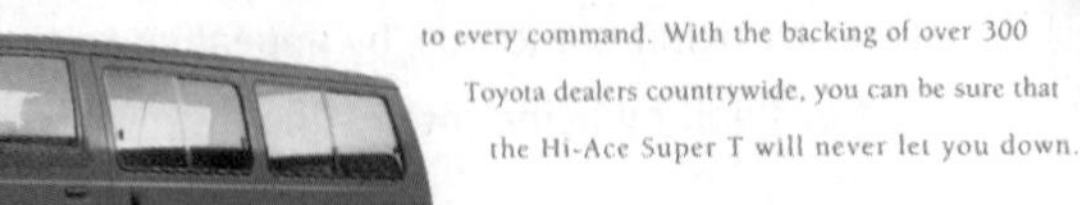

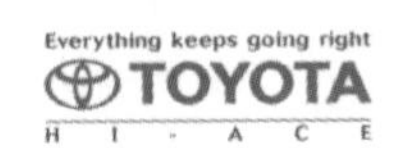
Everything keeps going right
TOYOTA
HI-ACE

LINDSAY SMITHERS-FCB T4019E

Chapter 25

BLACK ENGLISH – THE LANGUAGE ISSUE

If you've learnt a second language, you've probably been laughed at for pronouncing certain words incorrectly. I'm sure there'll be a few giggles here because of some of my sentence constructions. When I was a child, I couldn't for the life of me understand why the *ch-* in '*ch*emist' is pronounced differently from the one in '*ch*icken', and why 'dou*gh*' and 'enou*gh*' are pronounced differently.

The English language can be problematic in advertising and marketing, particularly between blacks and whites. *The Sowetan*, the biggest daily newspaper in the country with a circulation of over 206 000, gets little advertising according to John Campson and Moses Mmutlane, who are responsible for marketing the newspaper. White media planners that I spoke to agree with them. But they have their reasons, and one of them is the language issue. '*The Sowetan*'s articles are badly written,' they say. Moses is also aware of that charge, but has an answer for it: 'UK English is different from American English. And whites accept that. Yet they have a problem with accepting South African English. Who gives them the right to impose their English on us? What *The Sowetan* writes is South African English, and blacks can understand it.'

There is merit in Moses's argument. Language evolves. 'Whites are refusing to learn anything from us,' Moses continues, 'but we do learn from them. We can speak their languages and they can't speak ours. How many whites can speak Zulu or Sesotho? It's funny, isn't it?'

'Blacks love an open life,' he continued, 'whereas whites like a closed one. Blacks will read *Elle* magazine and the *Citizen* but whites won't read *The Sowetan*. If you're black and you read a black publication they see you as unsophisticated or earning a low income. They think that successful blacks live in Sandton and other such places. If you live in Soweto you are poor. The truth is there are people living in places like Diepkloof Extension. Those houses are bigger than some of the houses in the northern suburbs of Johannesburg. And their owners have either paid them off already or are close to doing so. They therefore have more disposable income than those who've just bought houses. The problem is that white marketers want to see themselves in you. They want you to mimic their lifestyle. You must dress like them, eat like them and speak like them, and only then will they think that you are successful.'

PRONOUNCING THE TOWNSHIP WAY

An accent is no plague, and everyone has got one. An accent is nothing more than the way in which you were taught to speak a language. Brands in the township are always pronounced and better understood in the township accent. My grandmother pronounced Jeyes Fluid as 'Jay's Flute', paper as 'pepper', Lemonade as 'Namanade'. I noticed that people of her age pronounced things that way. Were they wrong? I don't think so. I think consumers and brands have a common South African relationship. Consumers are the *baases*, and the brands are the maids. And as maids will tell you (and my grandmother was one for all her working life) a maid doesn't mind what the *baas* or missies calls her. She is only happy to earn her wage.

To communicate correctly, especially on radio, you have to find out exactly how your brand is pronounced, and you have to make sure that your voice-over artists pronounce those words as your target audience will understand them. Otherwise it stands no chance of being known or remembered, and that puts your advertising budget to waste.

Advertising is not a language lesson. It is putting your message across in such a way that the majority of your audience understands it. There is no use in using big words that only the educated élite will understand. This does not only apply to English but to African languages too.

I am Zulu-speaking, and learnt it for twelve years at school. However, when Zulu news comes up on television and radio, I can only understand about 70% of it. I am among the better ones. Some Zulu-speaking people have to wait for the English broadcast. It's not that Zulu is dying as a language, it's just that the SABC's editors are masters of waxing lyrical. With people moving around (in my case my grandfather left kwaZulu almost a hundred years ago), language changes.

In radio advertisements, make sure the voice-over artists pronounce the products like most black people; otherwise the target audience will not understand what the voice-over artist is talking about.

Some advertisements make the same mistake. They try to impress people with the language instead of impressing them with the product. Simple words are best. They let people concentrate on your thoughts rather than your individual words. A friend of mine, who was a copywriter, used to say, 'The smaller the mind of the writer, the bigger the words he uses in his ads.'

Business-to-business advertisements are the worst. Writers use jargon to show that they understand the client's products. And because the clients understand it, they take it for granted that other people in the industry do too. What they don't realise is that in many instances business decisions are not only made by the people who use the product. For instance, a CEO may play a part in choosing and buying equipment from a computer company and yet he may not be a computer fundi. The CEO must understand the adverts if he or she has to be convinced that your company is the best.

TRANSLATIONS

Boss: Zephania, why have you not been coming to work for the last two weeks? Do you know that's a fireable offence?'

Zephania: I was sick, *baas.*

Boss: Where's the doctor's certificate?

Zephania: I didn't go to the doctor, *baas.*

Boss: So how did you get cured?

Zephania: I went to the moon, *baas.*

Boss: To the moon? How did you get there?

Zephania: I walked.

Boss: You're fired.

This is an anecdote my English teacher used to tell to demonstrate how direct translation can ruin communication. Zephania went to the traditional doctor. And the Zulu word for traditional doctor is *inyanga,* which also means the moon.

Although Zephania's case is an extreme one, there are many instances where translated ads have an unintended effect. Most ads are conceived in English and then translated into the other ten official languages. In many instances the copywriters live in their own world and culture with their own idiosyncrasies. This leads to a diluted message. The best way to avoid this brand erosion is either to employ people who can speak the language or to employ excellent translators.

TRENDY LANGUAGE

Some marketers tend to think that by using fashionable language their ads sound cool. So they use slang in their ads.

The problem with slang is that it tends to be regional. Some words mean different things to different people. And unless you keep up with its fast rate of change, your brand can quickly become dated. When I was young, the word '*mpintshi*' meant a fool. But now it means 'friend'.

But slang is not a total no-no. It can suit certain brands, especially those targeted at the youth. But your ads can still be original and more effective if you minimise clichés and slang.

The difference between the correct letter and an almost correct one is the difference between a car and a cat.

With languages that have clicks such as Zulu and Xhosa, please use the correct ones. Some people think it is 'hip' to use incorrect clicks. I can't think of anything more irritating. If the right click is a '*c*', use a '*c*' and not a '*q*', and vice versa. For instance, do not use *caca* if the word is supposed to be *qaqa*. *Qaqa* is a skunk while *caca* means 'be clear'.

MARKETING CONSIDERATIONS

- Advertising is not a language lesson. It is about putting your message across in such a way that the majority of your audience understands you.
- Ideas based exclusively on English such as proverbs should be avoided unless they are well known.
- Language evolves. And communication should use current but acceptable language.
- There is no point in using mellifluous language in your communication.
- If you use trendy language in your communication, make sure that it is current.

26

KAFFIR, BANTU, PLURALS, NATIVES, PIKININS, WETSUITS, GOFFELS, WOGS, BUSH BUNNIES, KAFFIR, BANTU, PLURALS, NATIVES, PIKININS, WETSUITS, GOFFELS, WOGS, BUSH BUNNIES, KAFFIR, BANTU, PLURALS, NATIVES, PIKININS, WETSUITS, GOFFELS, WOGS, BUSH BUNNIES, KAFFIR, BANTU, PLURALS, NATIVES, PIKININS, WETSUITS, GOFFELS, WOGS, BUSH BUNNIES, KAFFIR, BANTU, PLURALS, NATIVES, PIKININS, WETSUITS, GOFFELS, WOGS, BUSH BUNNIES, KAFFIR, BANTU, PLURALS, NATIVES, PIKININS, WETSUITS, GOFFELS, WOGS, BUSH BUNNIES, KAFFIR, BANTU.

Chapter 26

POLITICALLY CORRECT ADVERTISING

I hate to use the term 'politically correct' because it has so many negative connotations. However, this has come as a response to both the derision and exclusion of certain communities in our society. For instance, people like me are no longer officially called 'Kaffirs' or 'Non-Europeans'. Women are no longer called the 'weaker sex', and more and more people realise that it's not right to call them 'cherries' either.

I find this complicated at times. Some words have become victims of our political history, like 'bantu'. A black professor once argued with me about that word.

This is how he advanced his argument:

Professor: What is the Zulu word for a Zulu?
Muzi: Zulu.
Professor: What is the word for someone who is a Xhosa?
Muzi: Xhosa.
Professor: Do you have any problem with the word Zulus?
Muzi: No.
Professor: Do you have any problem with the word Xhosas?
Muzi: No
Professor: Okay, what is the Zulu and Xhosa word for 'people'?
Muzi: Abantu.
Professor: So why do you have a problem with the word 'Bantus'?
Muzi: Because white people used it to discriminate against us, and they used it to humiliate us.
Professor: So if white people were to use your name to discriminate against you and to humiliate you, would you hate it?

Never mind about the rest of the argument. I lost it, I admit.

But unless you want to put your brand in serious trouble, you better not refer to black people as 'Bantus'.

Extreme political correctness ruins good communication.

Once I was walking with a white colleague of mine. A black boy of about 9 years approached us and asked for money. As a rule I don't give to street kids because when I was a child any adult who saw you begging was allowed to beat you. We were discouraged from having money because adults believed that it led to delinquency. The punishment would be even worse during school hours. (I remember being chased to school by an old man I didn't even know. I could tell by his accent that he was either from the Transkei or Ciskei. My crime: I was loitering during school hours. He chased me right into the school yard. Can you imagine the embarrassment? Anyway, I thank the old man wherever he may be.)

Back to Roeland Street with my white colleague. When he saw me refusing to give the street kid money, he also refused. But I could see the poor soul was torn between pleasing me and doing what he always does. A few hours later he asked me: 'Do you really think that that gentleman felt offended that I didn't give him any money?'

'Which gentleman?'

'That young one who asked us for money earlier.'

I could understand his problem. The word 'boy' has bad connotations when used in reference to black people. But the word 'gentleman' is equally inappropriate when used to address a 9-year-old!

This ex-colleague of mine is a copywriter. And this fear of offending black people is deeply embedded. Another copywriter once asked me whether to spell 'black people' with capitals or not. I asked him, 'How do you write "white people"?' 'With small letters,' he replied. 'I think you should do the same with "black people,"' I replied. There is a big, fat line between respect and paranoia. Paranoia leads to tasteless advertising at best and overt insincerity at worst.

MARKETING CONSIDERATIONS

- Avoid what people consider to be derogatory words.
- Extreme political correctness can ruin good communication.

CONCLUSION

As I finish writing this book, I am reminded of a white guy I know who, having discovered that I am in advertising, asked me how to go about marketing his business in the black market. It was a year before the 1999 election. He was going to start a coffin-manufacturing company. But his was to be different. People could pay in advance for their coffins, which would be delivered to keep at home. And the 1999 election was going to kick-start his business because of the forecasted violence. And with so many people being HIV positive, his business would grow tremendously.

I refused to help him because I have faith in this country and its people. And every day my faith is reaffirmed by the millions who get on buses, trains and taxis to go to work.

Lately, increasing crime, disease and interest rates are causing justified desperation. But I still have faith. And faith doesn't have to be justified. My future depends on South Africans spending their hard-earned money on bread, books, alcohol, savings or investment accounts or anything else that keeps our economy going.

If you are in marketing, advertising or any other industry, you must have faith. Irrational as it may be. Sometimes it will waver and when that happens remember those people who stock-piled tons of food, water and petrol before our first democratic election. They were all wrong. And history, as they say, repeats itself. Even with positive things.

ENDNOTES

CHAPTER 1

1 'Mawe' means Ma. But in fact she is *mamkhulu,* or my mother's elder sister.
2 Gogo means 'grandmother' in Zulu.
3 Senior mother.

CHAPTER 2

1 Town could be anyplace that was designated a white area during apartheid.

CHAPTER 3

1 'FMCG' – fast moving consumer goods.

CHAPTER 4

1 Shebeen comes from Irish - a house selling alcohol illegally.
2 Bottle store is South African English for any shop trading in wine, malt and spirits.
3 'Bra' (from 'brother') is a prefix denoting respect for a man.

CHAPTER 10

1 Pet name meaning 'my dumpling'.
2 Small legs.

CHAPTER 12

1 Kwaito is a form of township music.

CHAPTER 18

1 Source: Adindex. Note that these figures are rounded figures. Figure excludes trade newspapers and weeklies.
2 At the time of writing this, a consortium is bidding to buy Kaya FM.

CHAPTER 19

1 *Sunday Times,* 13 June 1999.

CHAPTER 23

1 *Business Today.* Radio 702, 4 May 1999.

ACKNOWLEDGEMENTS

Aunt Thokozile walked into my mother's house as I was writing the last chapter of this book. The discussion quickly changed into politics and religion, as it usually happens in townships. 'The Devil', she said, 'was expelled from heaven not for adultery, fornication, murder or any such ghastly sin, but for pride. That's all.' To try and secure my place in heaven, and because in Africa we sing a man's praises while he is still alive so that he can hear them, I'd like to humble myself and say 'thank you' to the following:

Bob Rightford, Karin Watling, Ian Calver and Jono Shubitz for believing in me.

The people who had the patience to train me how to write advertising copy: Matthew Bull, Greg Burke, Alastair King, Alan Raaff and Brian Searle-Tripp (thank you for striking the match when it was dark, Brian).

Those who either trained or inspired me in different ways or simply gave me the opportunity to try my hand: Chris Charles, Kobus Conradie, Bryan Gibson, Margaret Gibson, Mike Goode, Pam Haddad, Rob Hill, Sue Hoffman, Craig Irving, Yvonne Johnstone, Mike Joubert, Washiela Kappery, Gary May, Arthur Mzozoyane, Nyakale Mokgosi, Bruce Paynter, Don Paul, Gavin Pieterse, Prea Pillay, Lee le Roux, Christine Stearman and Denise van der Westhuizen.

There are many people who helped in putting this book together either by providing material, granting me interviews or pointing me in the right direction: Catherine Airey, Ian Bennet, Helen Casey, Hendrick Chiloane, Amanda Economides, Dirk Hartford, Rori Maclean, Alain Main, Moses Mmutlane, Kaibe Mollo, Alvin Nadas, Mary Ngubane, Joe Speelman, Dave St. Quinton, Ian Taylor, Pula Tongane, Deon Viljoen, Bra Peter Vundla (thank you for inspiring a whole lot of blacks) as well as the numerous people who asked me not to reveal their identity. Andrew Birrel, Mike Roux, Neil Horne.

I'd also like to thank the following advertising agencies for their assistance: Berry Bush BBDO, TBWA Hunt Lascaris, Ogilvy and Mather, and Herdbuoys McCann Erickson.

I owe special gratitude to Father Dominic Baldwin who knew about the dream even before I woke up to tell him about it, and taught me many useful things.

Special thanks to Senne Bogatsu, Professor Sonya Grier and Mike Teke for their insightful contributions.

Finally I must pay the greatest tribute to Maggie Davey. I walked into David Philip looking for a publisher and ended up with a friend.

ACKNOWLEDGMENTS